CDL MINDED BUSINESS

STARTUP STRATEGY
—— COLLECTION ——

3-Step System to Leverage Time, Have Unlimited Freedom and
Maximize Security in the CDL Industry while Building, Establishing,
and Growing Your Brand in Your Business for Entrepreneurs, Small
Business Owners, and Commercial Driver/Operators

JOE RYDER & Eric Balma

Interior design by FormattedBooks

CDL Business Productivity GAME PLAN

Entrepreneurs Guide to Quick Start your Business to the Next Level

Thank you! Here's a Free Gift! For You :)

As a special thanks from me to you, you'll receive:

- ❏ 3 Powerful Elements of Productivity in your Business
- ❏ 5 Simple Strategies to Mastering Productivity in your Business
- ❏ The Highest Quality of Productivity Charts
- ❏ Valuable Resources that you Must Know and much more!

To receive your Free copy of the CDL Business Productivity GAME PLAN, you can go to my website at:

cdlforlife.com/cdl-business-resources

SCAN ME   **SCAN ME**
(For your Free Business Game Plan)   (If you want my Books for Free)

Also If you would like to get my books for Free and before anyone else, go to my website at:

cdlforlife.com/cdl-business-resources

Table of Contents

CDL MINDED ENTREPRENEUR

STEP 1: CDL-Minded Starts With YOURSELF

STEP 2: CDL-Minded in YOUR 'Business'

STEP 3: Living the CDL-Minded Lifestyle

CDL MINDED MARKETING

CDL MINDED ENTREPRENEUR

3-STEP SYSTEM TO LEVERAGE TIME,
HAVE UNLIMITED FREEDOM AND MAXIMIZE SECURITY IN THE CDL INDUSTRY

JOE RYDER

Introduction

Before becoming an entrepreneur in the CDL industry, work was just something I did to pay the bills. Coming home on the verge of exhaustion used to be just another day for me. I would walk in the front door with hardly enough energy to stumble over to the couch, as the aches and pains of the day and my long schedule caught up with me. I barely had the energy to watch half an episode of TV before I fell asleep halfway from the couch to the bedroom, let alone having enough energy to spend quality time with my family. I was working myself to the bone, all for wages that only barely covered all of my expenses. The worst part of it all was that I knew I would just have to do it all again the next day. It seemed like there was no end in sight.

This is probably a familiar story to many of you. Work can dominate your life, even and especially if you're not making enough money to be able to save some. If your job is routine, menial work, it becomes even harder to dedicate so much of your life to it. This is the life that so many people lead, but that doesn't mean it's the only option. After living this way for years, I decided that it wasn't how I wanted to live the rest of my life. I didn't want work to take up such a large portion of my day that I didn't have any time for my family. I didn't want to be so tired that my hobbies and passions fell by the wayside. I didn't want to struggle with my finances, trying to decide whether or not I could afford a new pair of shoes this week, or if I had to wait until my next payday. I was tired of being tired, and I knew if I wanted my life to change, it had to start with my job.

Becoming an entrepreneur in the Commercial Driver's License (CDL) and commercial trucking industry was my ticket out. When I made the decision to become a CDL entrepreneur, so many things in my life changed. I set my own hours and had more time away from work so that I could spend time with my family more often. As my business grew bigger and more successful, I had more money, so I wasn't always worrying about financial troubles. I found that commercial trucking was my passion, and I felt more fulfilled doing work

I really cared about. I found I had more control over my life, and that sense of control helped me feel more content with my life as a whole. My life was entirely changed by this decision, and yours can change too.

You can have a job that you really care about and that you excel in. You can be your own boss, choose when you want to work and when you want to take time off, and experience more freedom both in the workplace and in your personal life. You can live on a comfortable income, and free yourself from the constant stress that money-trouble creates. When you become an entrepreneur in the CDL industry, you get to call the shots and regain control over your life.

Building your own business is never an easy process, and the CDL industry is no exception. However, if you develop the right mindset and become "CDL-Minded," you can practically guarantee future success. When you start thinking like an entrepreneur, it becomes easy to expand your company into a profitable business. With CDL-Minded Entrepreneur, you will learn how to make smart and wise business decisions in a lucrative marketplace. I will help you devise a plan for establishing and developing your company. I will also walk you through the process of developing the mindset you need in order to make your CDL business a success so that you can enjoy personal and financial freedom.

Driving and operating a truck driving business is a labor of love for me. It is an industry that is so important to me, and one that I genuinely love working in. I know the ins and outs of the commercial driving business because it has been a part of my life for over 25 years. I have been a commercial operator, business entrepreneur, truck driver, and instructor to many students. I operated my own multi-million dollar business, and I have taught my students how they can achieve the same level of success. This is life-changing information, as my students have gone on to earn at least $60,000 to $100,000 a year with their own businesses. They have told me that they cannot imagine starting and maintaining a business without the critical guidance I have provided, especially the three-step system, which you too will learn.

What you're about to discover has been a closely guarded secret kept by many Fortune 500 companies. The CDL trucking industry will never tell you these secrets, but I will unveil the way you can drastically increase your profits and your chances of long-term, lasting success. I will take you, step-by-step, through the process of creating and sustaining a truly profitable company. I believe that everyone, not just the wealthy elite, should have the opportunity to reach this level of success, and I want to help you achieve it. By following my strategies, you could make enough money to retire in as little as five years, secure in the knowledge that you'll never need to work another day in your life if you don't want to. You will be able to live far beyond your current financial means. Rather than being trapped by the daily grind at work, you will experience unlimited freedom in your new life as an entrepreneur in the commercial trucking industry.

It's time for you to make the same change in your life that I made in mine. It's time to start your own company in the CDL industry and enjoy all of the wealth and freedom that comes with it. You will face some challenges, but if you are really committed to improving your quality of life, you won't let that hold you back. When you start thinking about the road ahead as an exciting new opportunity, you'll soon find that all of the challenges were worth the amazing results. If you want to run a successful business that ensures you'll never have to miss out on family time or worry about your financial situation again, you need to become a CDL-Minded Entrepreneur.

STEP 1

CDL-Minded Starts With YOURSELF

CHAPTER 1

Making the Decision and Applying the CDL-Minded Habits

Becoming a CDL entrepreneur is much more than a simple career change. If you really want to be an effective CDL business owner, you must step out of the mindset of the typical employee. No matter what your previous job was, owning your own business is a big step. It's going to require you to turn your thinking around and really embrace the idea of thinking like an entrepreneur. This will also require you to adopt CDL-Minded habits to ensure your success. But what does a CDL-Minded approach really mean?

Being CDL-Minded means more than just taking on additional responsibilities. It means thinking, feeling, and acting like you're a professional in the CDL industry. If you want to make it big, you'll want to go in with a mindset that promotes success. You need to believe that you will be successful before you even take your first few steps. Having a confident, forward-thinking mindset will give you the passion you need to start this new life journey, and the tenacity you need to see it through even when times get tough. It is not enough to just work like an entrepreneur; you must think and live like an entrepreneur.

This change in your mindset doesn't happen overnight. It takes dedication to start thinking this way, especially if you are used to working for others and just putting in the required effort to get your job done. You're going to have to start actively seeking out opportunities and rethinking the way you approach your job. Changing your mindset also requires clarity on your goals and dreams. This begins with some self-discovery so you can understand just what your life's purpose is and why it matters to you. This process influences your mission statement and vision for the future. It will also help you start adopting healthy, ambition-driven habits that allow you to set and achieve your goals. When you understand what you want, and you spend time training yourself into the mindset of a successful entrepreneur, it becomes much more likely that you will actually become a successful entrepreneur in the CDL industry.

Finding Your Life's Purpose

Our life's purpose is the reason why we're here on this earth. Finding our purpose gives our very existence meaning. It is what we should strive to accomplish every day. Without knowing our purpose, we might wander around blindly through life, moving from job to job, toiling away under someone else's thumb for years. We could waste our precious time doing a job we hate that isn't suitable for our lifestyle. If we want to feel fulfilled in life, we must find and pursue our life's purpose.

Of course, this information isn't easy to come by. Many people go their whole lives without finding something they're passionate about. In order to understand your life's purpose, you need to take some time to really think about what your ideal life would look like. It requires a lot of self-reflection and visualization. Are you relaxing on a beach, enjoying personal comforts, and no longer stressing out over financial concerns? Do you have a big, loving family with plenty of kids and grandkids? Do you volunteer or otherwise support people in your community? Do you wake up in the morning each day excited for your job, and if so, what job is it?

Answering these kinds of questions by visualizing your ideal future can help you understand the value of your life and how you can achieve self-fulfillment. In order to arrive at these answers, you must have a deep understanding of yourself, your needs, and your desires. It is only then that you can start to effectively pursue your goals.

The Importance of Knowing Your Purpose

What happens if we go through life without a purpose? Would it really be so bad? As previously mentioned, it's not something that everyone realizes during their lives. Surely, you might think we could live without taking all this time for self-reflection. We very well might be able to live, but simply living is different from thriving. We can go through the motions, but feelings of self-fulfillment will continue to elude us.

Rather than being fully present each day, we go on a sort of autopilot through life. Our days are made up of the same dull routine, and we continue going through the motions without really taking note of what we are doing. We know that there's more to life than this, but we don't really feel the need to achieve anything else, or if we do, it's only for the sake of making ourselves more comfortable. Most people shy away from opportunities that require them to work a bit harder for a bigger reward because they don't see them as being steps to a better life. They lack the ambition required to do something really daring and different, which means they just do the work others tell them to do. This kind of mindset can keep us from venturing out into becoming an entrepreneur.

When we take time to discover and understand our life's purpose, we also discover a reason to leave our previous lives behind and aim for a better quality of life. We find a drive and motivation that encourages us to get up and get moving. This makes it possible for us to take the daring and often scary leap into becoming an entrepreneur. There will be a lot of uncertainty, but if we are working towards our life's purpose, we won't let that stop us. In fact, there's very little that will stop us when we find the proper motivation in life.

No one ever became successful by living a completely unchallenged life. It is impossible to go through life without facing challenges, whether they appear in our careers or our personal lives. When we encounter these challenges, we have two options. We can let valuable opportunities pass us by and decide that the trouble is not worth the reward, shrug, and back down from the challenge. If we choose this path, we'll never make any progress towards our goals.

On the other hand, we can look at these challenges as chances to better ourselves and get closer to what we want. When we start seeing them as stepping stones leading towards our long-term goals, it is much easier to take them on, not just begrudgingly, but with genuine passion and feeling. We can see how each challenge fits into the bigger picture, and the desire to avoid difficulties in life starts to fade away as we plan for bigger and better things.

Being a CDL entrepreneur means facing plenty of challenges each day. It means trying to build a new company from the ground up. It means learning new skills necessary for running a business, such as accounting, people skills, and having a good nose for business. If you previously worked in a different industry, it might even mean learning all about the CDL industry and the ways that you can make your company stand out and find success. However, if all of these challenges are standing in the way of achieving your life's goals, they won't be such big roadblocks after all. You'll find yourself ready and even eager to take them on, as doing so brings you closer to what you really want in life. You will find yourself freed from the chains of uncertainty and living on autopilot, ready to keep moving in life no matter what comes next. So long as you can find the motivation to keep going, it is only a matter of time before you achieve personal and professional success in the CDL industry and in your life as a whole.

How to Identify and Apply Your Life's Purpose

Even after you know how important having a purpose is, it can still be hard to identify the unique goals and interests that appeal to you. When you try to picture your ideal future, your mind might draw a blank. There are so many possible paths our lives can take, with many different outcomes. How do we even begin deciding on the outcome we want to achieve, and once we do, how do we get there?

If you're stumped, try narrowing your scope a bit. Rather than trying to decide what you want your entire future to look like, focus on more specific details like your financial situation and your family. First, identify the parts of your life that bring you dissatisfaction. Look for areas where you feel unfulfilled or times when you felt exhausted and worn down. Next, think about how you could improve upon these areas. From there, you can get a better picture of what matters to you and how you can start working to achieve these goals. Ideally, you also want to begin considering how becoming an entrepreneur in the CDL industry can help you reach your full potential.

Even with this narrowed focus, looking to the future can be tough. It helps to break down your goals into three different areas: what you want for yourself, what you want for your family, and what you want for your community group or culture.

Start with the things you want for yourself in your life. Think about what you'd like to achieve in areas such as your dream job, your ideal financial situation, and your current or future family. If you could lead any life you wanted to, what would it be? Do you want a fast-paced job, where every day presents you with a new challenge you get to solve, or would you rather have a slow, relaxed life that is more focused on your personal relationships than your career? Are you looking to build up a nice financial cushion to coast on comfortably, or are you interested in becoming truly wealthy? Do you want a big family with kids, or do you not have any immediate plans for expanding your current family? Identifying what *you* want should come first before you worry about what others may want from you.

Once you know what your own personal goals are, you can consider if your current lifestyle is helping you achieve these goals, or if you need to make some changes. You should also take a moment to consider how becoming a CDL entrepreneur ties back into these personal goals. If you want to start living comfortably, but you always find yourself facing money troubles, starting your own CDL business can help you increase your income. If you want to be able to spend more time with your kids, running your own business can provide you with the freedom to choose your own hours. This gives you more free time to share with your family.

Consider personal goals that involve developing and cultivating certain personal values as well. You might want to build greater self-confidence, work on your charisma, improve your interpersonal skills, or refine any number of areas where you feel you have limited experience. Making improvements to these kinds of skills can help you become a more well-rounded person while also supporting your pursuit of your other goals. Becoming a CDL entrepreneur can help with developing these skills too.

As you start taking charge in your own company, you will become better at managing conflicts and thinking critically about a problem to arrive at an effective solution. Inspiring confidence in your business means acting confidently yourself, and the more experience you get putting yourself into uncertain situations, the easier it becomes to accept that risk is just a part of success. Taking note of how the experiences you will gain as a CDL entrepreneur can contribute to all of your personal goals, will help you remain motivated throughout the process of establishing and running your own company.

Next, consider your life's purpose in terms of your family. What do you want for your family? What kinds of lives do you want to help your kids lead? This is a little different than thinking about what you want your family to look like. Instead, you should consider what kind of goals you can achieve together and how you can set them up for success. Maybe you want to save enough money so your children's college expenses are covered. Maybe you want your kids to come work with you in your future CDL business when they're old enough, or you want to show them the value of hard work in life no matter what their dreams are. You might also have goals related to things you and your spouse can achieve together, like good communication and caring deeply about each other, or perhaps working together in this new entrepreneurial venture in your life.

Finally, think about how your life's purpose relates to your community and culture. How can you improve the lives of those around you? Why does it matter to you that your community is improved? Think about the charitable causes that matter most to you, which are often those that have had a direct impact on your life. Some people get involved in fundraising for cancer research centers because they have lost a relative to cancer. Others work to support their local food banks because they know what it is like to go hungry.

Once you've identified a positive change you can make in your community, consider how you can best support these efforts. Sometimes this means volunteering to help out at a fundraising or awareness-raising event. Other times it might mean donating some money or goods where they are needed most. While there are countless ways you can get involved right now, becoming a CDL entrepreneur can help you make an even bigger impact. It can give you the flexible schedule and free time you need to be able to volunteer, or the extra savings that you can donate to help others. By improving your own life, you can improve the lives of many others.

Charity work isn't the only way you can support your community. You might find that pursuing a hobby with your newfound free time and developing your skills in a creative pursuit, like art or writing, can help too. Even just reaching out and talking to others in your community, trying to foster a genuine connection, can help you make a positive impact on your neighbors. Doing some good in the world, no matter how you choose to do it, can help you feel like you are living a more fulfilling life and show you the value of your efforts in improving the lives of others.

Overall Mindset Approach

Our life's purpose should inform and influence our overall mindset. When we know what we want to do with our lives, it becomes much easier to convince ourselves that we are capable of doing it. Focusing on our goals gives us a positive mindset that encourages us to take action and work towards the results we want to see. Setting specific goals and understanding how our choices make an impact on our ability to achieve these goals is imperative. Our desire to achieve our long-term goals gives us the strength we need to leave our current jobs behind and pursue becoming a CDL entrepreneur.

If we don't set goals in line with our purpose in life, we can have trouble shaking ourselves out of our daily routine, even if the current routine is unfulfilling. We might continue living our lives aimlessly, just taking one day at a time and never seeing how valuable each day can be for getting closer to our goals. When we set goals, we subconsciously remind ourselves that we are capable of improving the things that bring us dissatisfaction in life. Our lives become a pathway towards our goals, which makes us more likely to take a risk or make a big career change.

Breaking our goals down into individual, family, and community goals demonstrate how each type of goal feeds into the next. The goals we set at an individual level are instrumental in achieving our family-oriented goals, which in turn help us achieve our community goals. Saving money for our children's education is only possible if we achieve the financial freedom we desire. We can only donate any excess money to charitable causes we are passionate about if we have first made sure our families are well taken care of. If we want to help our communities, we must first help ourselves. Achieving our individual goals gives us both the ability and the drive to achieve other life goals.

Setting short-term and long-term goals is key for success. We need to adopt a goal-oriented mindset if we want to fulfill our purpose in life. Keeping our goals in mind helps us make decisions that bring us closer to success and fulfillment. It also helps keep us motivated when we face difficult challenges. When striking out as an entrepreneur, you will face plenty of difficulties, whether they come in the form of learning how to build a company from scratch, managing employees, dealing with finances, or any number of other possible issues. However, when you are focused on achieving your goals, it becomes much easier to take these challenges in stride. If you care about the product of your work, it hardly feels like work at all.

Mission and Vision Statements

Part of understanding your purpose is understanding your vision for the future and your mission statement, both as an individual and for your future company. Your mission and vision statements should be a representation of who you are, what you stand for, and what you work to achieve as a whole. It should reflect what matters most to you and guides your actions.

If your vision for yourself is to be more optimistic and always look for silver linings on dark clouds, you should try to reexamine negative and self-defeating thoughts when they appear. If your vision for your company is to provide top-quality service, the way your company functions should prioritize giving customers this high-quality experience. In other words, your mission statement is the way that you provide unique value to yourself, your family, your community, and to the marketplace. It is what helps you stand out from the crowd and build a more personal relationship with your community and your customers alike.

Developing a clear idea of your mission statement will help you keep your focus on the future. It will also help you make tough choices where you need to prioritize one service at the expense of another. Ideally, you'd want your company to provide a service that is quick, high-quality, and low-cost, but sometimes this just isn't possible, especially when you are just starting out. You might need to sacrifice a bit of quality in order to get things moving faster, or you might need to charge more if you're focusing on providing the best possible service. If you know your company's mission statement, you can make a choice that matches your priorities. Many companies can charge more for a speedy premium service, while others do their business by being quick and cheap, even if the end results are a little rushed. Think of a business like Walmart, which is known for having slightly lower quality products but which offers some of the lowest possible prices. Alternatively, customers who care more about quality are likely to shop at more specialty stores, but at a greater cost for most products. The differences between a big-box retailer like Walmart and a specialty boutique come from differences in their mission statements.

What you choose to prioritize in your own company will depend on what kind of service you want to provide. A mission statement that promises customers speedy service first and foremost should prioritize that above all else; the same is true of companies that promise quality or low prices. The decisions you make as you begin to establish your CDL company and the actions you take now to expand your business will be a product of your mission statement and your vision for the future of your company.

How to Apply Your Mission and Vision Statements

Applying your mission and vision statements is a similar process to applying your life's purpose. They both help guide your decisions and give you the motivation to pursue your long-term goals. Just like you did with your life's purpose, you can break down your mission statement into your individual vision, your vision for your family, and your vision for your community or culture group.

Write out your individual vision or personal mission statement first. It is a representation of who you are as a person and what you want to accomplish. It should include both your purpose and how you want to achieve that purpose. Try to include your skills, your personality traits, and the dreams and passions that you want to pursue. For example, maybe you highly value helping others reach their goals. Your mission statement might say that you want to be a teacher for others and that you want to show them how they can be successful and encourage their growth. You might value giving each client the best possible service and a personal yet professional experience. Your mission statement can be something like trying to always learn more every day and growing as a person, or trying to be someone your friends and family can rely on in a crisis.

Once you've identified your personal vision, take steps to fulfill your promise to yourself. Teaching others means finding your own success first, then sharing that knowledge as a mentor figure. Prioritizing amazing service might mean you have to work a little harder than your peers, but if you're really committed to providing the best service for customers, the extra work will be worth it. Being reliable means helping others out even when it inconveniences you. You may need to make sacrifices or tough decisions in many of these examples, but you will feel more personally fulfilled if you stick to your individual mission statement.

Next, write out your mission statement for your family. What should your family value most above all other things? What standards should you keep for how you interact with each other and how you behave towards others? Maybe you want your family to be loving and supportive of each other. Maybe you want to share a lot of quality time and really come together. Having a family mission statement can help your family push back against some common but potentially harmful societal trends. Therefore, creating your own culture of caring for each other is one of the most healthy ways to keep a family together. Focusing on family bonding is another way to keep kids out of trouble and even deepen the relationship between yourself and your significant other.

Your family culture should take into account the goals of all of your family members. When in doubt, talk to your family and ask them what they feel is missing. Do your kids feel like you are a present parent, or is too much of your time spent at work? Do they feel like they can talk to you about their struggles? Though it may not initially seem like it, becoming an entrepreneur can help you live along the guidelines established by your family mission statement. For example, having more control over your schedule can help you spend more time with everyone. With a little more money in your savings, you could go on that family vacation you've been putting off. The simple act of allocating more time for your family can show them you really care and help you all grow closer.

Finally, write your mission statement for your culture or community. What kind of service do you want to provide to your community, and why does providing that service matter to you? It is easy to get wrapped up in caring about ourselves, but when we expand our focus and care about the well-being of others, we often feel better about ourselves in return. A mission statement that prioritizes your community might involve a dedication to community service, or a desire to operate in a way that supports your area by hiring locally and making sure your employees are being treated fairly.

These kinds of goals can be achieved by making donations with a company or personal profits or volunteering your time. You might also choose to be very vocal about issues that matter to you in order to raise awareness. Having a successful business can help with this too—when celebrities and successful entrepreneurs speak out on issues, their large audience turns the issue into a talking point, which can lead to more donations or public support. These kinds of actions often have the added benefit of more public support for your business, too, as people come to see you as a charitable company.

Overall Mindset Approach

Your personal mission statement and the mission statement you create for your business should work in tandem to help you accomplish your goals. They should both influence your overall mindset and keep you striving for positive change at all times. Vision statements give you purpose and direction. They help you choose a course and stick to that course, and they guide you through otherwise tough decisions. Trying to achieve your vision statement with every decision you make with your business trains your brain to prioritize the things that will get you closer to your long-term goals.

Your vision statement should also influence the working environment of your business. When you first start out, you will probably only have a handful of people working for your business, but as you continue to grow, you will have many employees. If you maintain a clear mission statement and make sure that your employees are aware of your company mission, they are more likely to share the same values in their work. If employees get the sense that their company doesn't care about the quality of their work, they won't care about it either. On the other hand, a company that prioritizes quality work will train its employees to prioritize quality work too. Mission and vision statements are critical to fostering a positive and productive mindset for both yourself and your employees.

Long-Term Health

If you want to be successful, you need to get and stay healthy. Poor health habits jeopardize your chances of reaching your goals. A health scare could mean you need to take time off from work, or you could become completely unable to do certain tasks without putting your well-being at risk. Overworking yourself to the point of exhaustion could result in your work quality and productivity suffering. Your health is just as important as your mindset.

Taking a long-term view of your goals and your mindset also means taking a long-term view of your health. The small things you do every day that improve or hurt your health, add up over time. Grabbing a donut for breakfast or working late into the night to finish up a stressful project aren't great things to do for your health, even if they are only small lapses in judgment. You might be tempted to brush these things off as barely a drop in the bucket of your overall health, and if they only happened once or twice they might not have a big effect. However, if you repeat these bad health habits too often, they can become a much bigger problem. Looking at your health in the long-term means recognizing that actions and choices, that seem harmless at the moment, can actually be more damaging than you might think. They represent a pattern of bad behavior that can sneak up on you if you're not careful.

Don't just worry about your physical health either. While good physical health is something you should always strive for, your mental, emotional, and social health all play a role in your overall well-being too. Maintaining good mental health supports a positive, goal-oriented mindset. If you get too worndown or you start thinking overly critically about yourself, you can become completely unmotivated, giving up on your goals and holding yourself back from success.

Your emotional health has to do with how you manage difficult emotions. If a temporary setback occurs and you feel upset or frustrated, what do you do with those feelings? If you allow them to overwhelm you, you impede your progress towards your goals. If you can properly manage anger, sadness, and the fear of failure, you will find it easier to recover from setbacks. Your social health is important too. Socializing isn't just a good idea for networking; it's also integral to your health. If you don't spend enough time with friends and family, you can get very burned out in your work very quickly. Managing all four of these aspects of your health is important if you want to achieve your goals.

Why Your Health Matters

The healthier we are, the easier it is to focus on our work and be productive. If we let negative emotions pile up, we can start doubting our abilities and talk ourselves out of new opportunities. If we eat poorly and don't exercise, we could put our physical health in jeopardy, which might lead to serious medical conditions. If we neglect our mental health and spend too much time working alone, not only do our productivity levels suffer (as well as our moods), but our families, communities, and businesses suffer as well when we don't take care of the only human vehicle we have: our bodies. Therefore, staying mentally, emotionally, socially, and physically healthy enables us to overcome these barriers and stay on track towards success.

Maintaining good long-term health ties into your happiness formula, which is "the unique mix of environmental factors and activities that are most likely to invigorate you and reset your energy batteries when they are running low" (Blake, 2017, para. 7). Maximizing your happiness formula involves fulfilling both your micro, daily needs and your macro, long-term needs. For example, something like taking a walk might be a micro need for your physical and mental health, while getting regular exercise would be a macro need. Spending some time with friends over the weekend is a micro need, while having a good relationship with your friends and family is a macro need. Just as small bad habits can add up to a larger negative effect, so too can small good habits add up to achieving maximum happiness and fulfillment in your life. If your happiness formula is high, you will be more productive and focused at work and at home.

How Your Health Applies to Your Goals

Good physical, mental, emotional, and social health allows us to get more done and get closer to achieving our goals. If you're in a terrible mood, your thoughts are cluttered, and you're feeling unmotivated, it can feel impossible to get started on a task. This is especially true if that task isn't something particularly fun. Your thoughts might keep leaping to all the other things you could be doing, making the current task take longer. You might become frustrated more easily, letting minor annoyances become major roadblocks that halt your progress. A task that should only take a matter of minutes ends up taking hours, or it gets ignored and forgotten until you can no longer put it off, forcing you to rush through it. Improving your health through the use of the happiness formula can help you refocus your mind, let go of agitation, and get some work done.

Think of your happiness and health needs like a mathematical equation. The happiness formula suggests that reaching maximum productivity is a matter of maximizing your happiness and ridding yourself of the things that are holding you back. This equation is "[(Ritual 1 + Ritual 2 + Ritual 3) x

Booster] – Barrier/s to Drop = Daily Happiness" (Blake, 2017, para. 13). In order to better understand how you can achieve your daily happiness, let's first break down this formula.

Your rituals are the things you need to do each day to support your health and happiness. These might be some light exercise, eating a home-cooked meal, practicing a hobby, or anything else that helps you feel energized and balances your emotions. The booster or multiplier is a daily habit that "supercharges" your energy levels. Finally, identify a barrier in your life that brings you stress or gets in the way of your work. These barriers might be anxieties you feel over future work, failure, money troubles, or other sources of worry. They might also be bad habits you engage in like eating junk food, procrastinating, or spending time around toxic people.

Now that you know what each term in the equation means, you can fill it out for a reliable pathway to achieving daily happiness. Choose three daily rituals to complete, add in a booster activity, and work to get rid of a source of stress, and you will find yourself living a happier life that supports a healthier lifestyle. Your happiness formula doesn't have to be set in stone; you can change up the daily rituals if you are looking for some more variety, or you find that the old ones aren't working for you. The most effective daily formulas will keep you happy and focused, letting you knock out your short-term goals and make progress towards your long-term goals every day.

Overall Mindset Approach

Our health plays a key role in our mindset. If we are distracted by negative thoughts and bad habits, we lay a shaky foundation for the rest of our attitude. Poor health takes its toll on our overall well-being. It becomes harder to achieve our goals when we haven't fulfilled our health needs, whether those needs are physical or emotional.

Making a commitment to taking care of our health in the short-term sets us up for long-term success. Daily healthy choices create a pattern of good habits. Every good choice we make improves our overall happiness and makes us more motivated and productive. As we keep repeating good habits, and we improve and maintain our health, we no longer have to worry about poor health, nor are we distracted by self-critical thoughts or over-whelming emotions. It becomes easier to focus on our goals and ultimately achieve them.

Lifestyle Habits for Success: Routine, Discipline, and Focus

Establishing and practicing good habits is integral to our ability to succeed. Just like daily healthy habits lead to more long-term success, so too do daily productivity and lifestyle habits. These habits should focus on three key qualities: routine, discipline, and focus. Through these qualities, we can improve our work ethic and bring ourselves closer to success.

Establishing Routines

Establishing a good, consistent daily routine is great for your productivity. You can start each day with a good idea of what you need to get done and when you need to complete it. Routines naturally reinforce good behaviors because you repeat them every day, turning them into long-lasting habits. Rather than being a chore that you might be tempted to procrastinate, it's second nature to sit down and get some work done around the same time each day. The same is true for other daily tasks like eating, sleeping, and exercising, as well as relaxation time. If you go to bed and wake up at different times every day, your body isn't always ready for sleep at night, which can lead to staring up at the ceiling when you should be asleep. You can become tired and cranky from this lack of sleep, not to mention how your work quality can suffer too. If you stick to a good sleeping routine instead, it becomes easier to fall asleep and wake up around the same time each day. You will be better rested, leaving you ready to tackle whatever the day has to offer. Try to stick to a similar schedule each day, and you will find that making good lifestyle choices becomes nearly automatic.

You might think to yourself, isn't part of the benefit of being your own boss the ability to work whenever you want? While it is true that you can set your own hours, you should still do your best to make sure the hours you set for yourself are consistent. If you give yourself all day to get a task done without setting aside certain hours as "working hours" and others as "leisure time," work and play bleed into each other. It's harder to focus on work when you keep thinking about more fun things you could be doing, and even harder if you constantly interrupt your train of thought by switching back and forth between your work and another activity. You can choose the hours that are most comfortable for when you like to work, but make sure that they remain as consistent as possible so you can get more work done during these hours.

Routines and other lifestyle habits also help us hold ourselves accountable for starting and finishing our work. Actor Denzel Washington once said, "Without commitment you will never start, but more importantly, without consistency you will never finish" (Washington, 2017). Routines, discipline, and focus are most effective when they are used consistently. Without consistency, you can't turn these behaviors into powerful lifestyle habits. Apply these habits every day and you will be able to finish any task, no matter how large. If we always get started at a certain time, we resist the urge to put something off for even an hour or two. This gives us more time to complete the task before we reach the end of the time we have set aside to work. Scheduling your day also keeps you from overworking yourself. It is easy to get lost in work and end up toiling away long into the night. Sticking to your self-scheduled "working hours" ensures that you still find time for leisure, even on your busiest days. It keeps burnout at bay while still giving you enough time to get all of your work done comfortably.

For the best routines, schedule your entire day, including your mornings, afternoons, and evenings. Set aside certain tasks for specific parts of the day. For example, your morning routine should help you wake up, get energized, and get focused. A good morning routine might involve a refreshing shower, a filling breakfast, some light exercise to get your blood moving, and then getting right to work. Your afternoon routine should be all about maintaining your momentum and resisting the afternoon slump. Get the most important tasks done first, so they are always completed by the end of the day, and make sure to eat a healthy lunch, taking breaks to stand and stretch as needed. In the evening, start wrapping up your work and transitioning over to leisure time. Resist the urge to work long into the night; you could throw off your sleep schedule and fail to get enough rest to be at the height of productivity the next morning. Stick to your schedule at all hours so you can maximize your productivity and keep working towards your goals.

Developing Discipline

Maintaining a good routine requires you to have a lot of discipline. Discipline can be a tricky thing to cultivate, especially when there are so many temptations to avoid. Our lives are full of potential distractions and unhealthy behaviors. These include anything from grabbing an unhealthy snack, to making impulse purchases that reduce your savings, to avoiding work because it seems too difficult. Without discipline, we allow our impulsive thoughts and our desires for instant gratification to get in the way of our long-term goals. We are tempted to pursue momentary pleasure at the expense of achieving success later on. We might shirk our work to do something more fun like hang out with friends or watch a movie, even though we know we are only hurting ourselves in the long run.

When these temptations arise, we need to have the discipline to say no and make the right decision. We have to resist caving to distractions, and we must remain focused on our goals. If we can manage to stay the course, we make the best use of our time. We also show ourselves just how far hard work can get us. Even if procrastinating our work might have been more fun, it wouldn't have brought us any closer to achieving our goals. Additionally, procrastinating often results in doing more work in the long run as you never really achieve a level of success that would bring you financial security. If you can stay disciplined and avoid temptations in all forms, it will be easier to keep what really matters in mind.

Sometimes improving self-discipline is just a matter of finding the right motivation. Temptations are so powerful because they promise us instant gratification. They offer a brief moment of happiness which seems enjoyable at the time but which doesn't hold a candle to the long-term happiness you can achieve by working towards your life's purpose. When you think about hitting the snooze alarm or putting off work for another hour, think of what your work is helping you achieve in the long term. Think of how it is contributing to your big life goals, and how if you don't get your work done, you won't be able to achieve what you really want in life. Remind yourself of the reason why you need to keep working towards your goals—whether that reason is for your family's sake, for your own sense of fulfillment, to find financial freedom, or any combination of these motivators—and you'll find that temptations that once seemed so strong don't have much power over you after all.

Sharpening Your Focus

CDL Business Productivity GAME PLAN

Entrepreneurs Guide to Quick Start your Business to the Next Level

Thank you! Here's a Free Gift! For You :)

As a special thanks from me to you, you'll receive:

❏ 3 Powerful Elements of Productivity in your Business
❏ 5 Simple Strategies to Mastering Productivity in your Business
❏ The Highest Quality of Productivity Charts
❏ Valuable Resources that you Must Know and much more!

Distraction is the enemy of hard work. If your mind is constantly elsewhere, or worse, if you get up and leave in the middle of work to satisfy an impulse, you interrupt your work and throw yourself off your schedule. Improving your focus can help you avoid caving to distractions. It can also help you get "in the zone" when you are working, which typically produces a higher quality result. The longer you maintain your focus on one task, the faster you will typically complete that task.

Our lives are full of distractions. There is always a new TV show or movie to watch that can steal a few hours from our workday. Other people might call our attention away from our work. We even carry distractions around with us in the form of our phones. While these devices might be necessary in the modern world, they also make it very easy to lose minutes or hours to endless scrolling on social media and other apps. If we want to maintain our focus in the face of these and other distractions, we need to find a way to block them out or remove them from our surroundings.

This might mean putting up a "do not disturb" sign when we are working on something important and letting others know that we are in the middle of something, and we can get back to them later. It might mean putting your phone on silent or turning it off so you aren't able to keep checking it. It could also mean removing sources of distraction like TVs and games from our workspace, so they can't catch our eye and tempt us. Cutting out these distractions allows us to keep our focus on our current task where it is needed most, helping us finish the task faster.

Multitasking is another form of distraction. Though it is often seen as a way to increase productivity, more often than not it actually makes you less productive because it interferes with your ability to give one task all of your attention. If you are constantly splitting your attention between two or more things, you never really get to focus on either one of them. You can reduce your working speed to a crawl and ruin the quality of your work as your mind struggles to repeatedly switch gears between the different tasks.

If you want to achieve maximum levels of productivity, focus on just one thing at a time. See that task through to its successful conclusion before taking on any other work. Even if you have multiple things you need to do in one day, take them one task at a time in order of greatest priority. It is only by keeping your focus narrowed to a single activity that you can get your work done with the greatest efficiency.

How to Apply Your Lifestyle Habits

Routines, discipline, and focus all play a role in keeping you on track to meet your goals. Without them, you will likely have trouble working efficiently and your productivity will suffer. When you learn to apply these positive lifestyle habits, you will notice a total change in the way you approach work. Instead of feeling like something you have to force yourself to do, work becomes something you might even feel excited to do.

These three key lifestyle habits all feed into each other. When combined, they greatly increase your ability to achieve success. Start out by writing down your daily routines. Plan out your day and make yourself a to-do list of the most important work that needs to get done. Next, apply discipline and focus to ensure you get your work done. Resist the urge to procrastinate work in favor of more "fun" activities. Reinforce your motivation to stick to your routine, and get your work done by thinking about how each task on your to-do list brings you closer to achieving your short-term and long-term goals.

The better you get at blocking out distractions, the more focused you will be as you work. Additionally, having a clear routine makes it easier to exercise restraint and avoid distractions. Tackling your work by utilizing a list reduces the chances of trying to multitask. It improves your focus by encouraging you to work on one thing at a time. When you apply each of these lifestyle habits, you provide yourself with a recipe for success.

Overall Mindset Approach

Big changes are the product of many smaller decisions. Adopting good lifestyle habits can turn a complex, difficult task into something more easily accomplished. Habits are an amazing way to get a little bit closer to your goals every day. You can use them to complete any large task that would otherwise feel overwhelming. If you get into the habit of making just a little progress towards a larger goal each day, you will eventually arrive at the finish line. Through using routines, developing discipline, and sharpening your focus, you can tackle many short-term goals on your way to greater success.

While it's important to always keep our long-term goals in mind, our short-term goals represent the steps on the path to these long-term goals. Like the positive habits we adopt in our daily lives, they help us make a little bit of progress towards becoming a successful CDL entrepreneur with enough money and control over our lives to accomplish even greater goals. These good habits show us how there is no goal too great for us to accomplish as long as we start small, think big, and build our way up to making a large-scale change in our lives.

The Power of Executing Smart Goals

Having goals is great, but taking the time to clearly define them and understand how you will go about achieving them is even better. Say your dream is to run your own business. If you never really develop your goal more than this, you aren't very likely to achieve it. Without setting up a clear timeline for achieving this goal, you might keep pushing it back, possibly never achieving it at all. Without fully understanding what the conditions for success are and what you would have to do to run your own company, you might assume much more work is required, or you might think the opposite and assume the task will be much easier than it actually is. Just like any assignment, you need to understand what is expected of you and how long you have to complete the task, even if the due date is only enforced by yourself. In order to set achievable goals, you must consider what you need to accomplish to get closer to your goal, develop a clear plan, and give yourself a deadline.

Proper planning goes a long way toward setting and achieving goals more efficiently. When you actually make an action plan for your long-term goals, you are much more likely to achieve them. In order to do this, you must learn to set and execute smart goals.

Setting smart goals helps you work smarter, not harder. According to Zig Ziglar, a successful salesman, author, and motivational speaker, the process of setting goals and successfully achieving them can be broken down into seven steps. His goal setting canvas outlines each of these steps and how they can help you create a plan of attack for even the most difficult goals. His steps include identifying the goal, listing the benefits of achieving the goal, listing the obstacles in your way, identifying the skills and knowledge you will need, looking for people who will help you achieve your goals, creating a step-by-step plan, and setting a deadline.

Identify the Goal

The first step in setting goals is deciding what you want to achieve. You need to set a target so you can aim towards that target in everything that you do. This step typically requires some self-reflection so you can identify your life's purpose and the goals that will help you be the person you want to be.

When identifying what you want in life, make sure you choose specific goals. As Ziglar says, "If you want to have specific success you must have specific targets" (Ziglar, n.d., para. 1). If you aim too broad, it will be difficult to know when you've achieved your goals. For example, saying that you want to become more productive is a good thing to aim for, but it's not a specific enough goal. What would being more productive look like for you? A better goal might be to commit yourself to getting your work done at the beginning of the day, or to double the amount of work you currently do. Similarly, wanting to have more money is another non-specific goal. Is having an extra dollar enough to qualify as "more money"? How can you tell? Pick something more specific, like setting a goal to have three months' worth of your current salary in your savings account. Specific goals give you something concrete to aim for and you get a clear idea of exactly when you have achieved your goal.

List the Benefits—What's in it for me?

Why does your goal matter to you? What really drives you to accomplish it? If you don't think that achieving your goal will help you, you won't have much motivation to keep working towards it. Listing out all of the benefits you will get from achieving a goal shows you why the goal is worth fighting for. These benefits might include financial freedom, more security for your family, or a sense of satisfaction and fulfillment.

It might initially feel a bit self-centered to wonder what's in it for you, but the truth is that your goals need to have personal significance. If you are trying to achieve them because it's what someone else expects you to do, you're not going to have the motivation you need to keep pushing for them when things get tough. Think of all the people who go to medical school or law school because their parents expect them to be doctors or lawyers, but who end up dropping out because they had no passion for the work they were doing. If you choose goals that you genuinely care about achieving and that bring you some personal benefit, you can push through even the toughest of obstacles in your path to success.

List the Obstacles to Overcome

No matter what you're trying to achieve, you're probably going to face some obstacles. While you can't predict everything, making a list of the most likely issues you will face will help you mentally prepare yourself for the challenge and devise a plan for overcoming them. It might seem like immediately listing out all the hardships you might encounter is a good way to demotivate yourself, but it's actually better to start working on your goals knowing that challenges are an unavoidable part of the process. If you let common problems blindside you and you fail to prepare for them, it is much harder to deal with them. If you know what could be coming, you can decide what you're going to do about it long before it ever becomes a problem.

If you're trying to break into the CDL field and start your own business, you will need to overcome some obstacles. For starters, you're going to need enough money to get the company off the ground. You could have some initial difficulties securing customers. You might have trouble finding enough employees to meet your customers' demands, or finding the right employees that fit in well with your company vision. It can take some time to reach a point where you are comfortable managing your company, and it's okay if you don't achieve immediate success. These issues are much easier to accept and deal with when you know about them in advance.

List the Skills and Knowledge Required

Now that you have a good idea of some of the obstacles keeping you from reaching your goal, think about the skills you would need to overcome these obstacles. Each goal requires a different skill set, as well as learning new information in a different area. The skills you need to cultivate if you want to learn to cook are very different from those you need to learn to run your own CDL business. Identify the skills and information that are the most important to your goal and take every opportunity to expand your abilities in these areas.

Identify the People and Groups to Work With

We can go very far on our own with enough self-discipline and skill, but not nearly as far as we can go with the help of others. Other people can lend us their skills and knowledge, allowing us to get more done and helping us in areas where we're not experts. Collaborators, mentors and advisors, team members, and employees can all assist us on our journey to success. Consider where your weaknesses lie and how other people can help you overcome these weaknesses.

When you run a business, you need to learn how to delegate. You aren't going to be able to do everything by yourself. Delegating involves finding the right person for every job, even and especially if that person isn't you. If you're not especially great at accounting, hire someone to deal with the company's finances. If you find you're spending far too much time on routine customer service, hire someone who can answer customer questions and provide them with the resources they're looking for. Even getting someone to answer the phone for you reduces the amount of time you waste each day, leaving you with more time to focus on the work that only you can do. Starting a company is a team effort. Fill your team with like-minded people and groups who will help you achieve your goals.

Develop a Plan of Action

You know what you need to do and you know the challenges you will face in your journey. It's time to develop your action plan for achieving your goals.

A good plan can save you a lot of trouble. In fact, making a plan is the most important step in the process of making smart goals. Without one, you have a goal in mind but no idea how you're going to get there. Think of it like getting in the car with a destination in mind but no instructions for how to get there. You could waste plenty of time driving around in circles and taking the wrong exits. Your plan is like the GPS that guides you towards your destination, always keeping you on the right track. Once you have your GPS, you can simply follow its instructions; you don't have to worry if every turn you make is the right one because you've already planned out your journey.

To write out your plan, think about the details of how you will achieve your goal. Look at the big steps you'll have to take, then break them down into the small steps that contribute to the bigger ones. For example, if one of your big steps is getting enough money to start your company, the smaller tasks might include researching how much money you will need, running a fundraiser, looking for investors, and taking out personal loans to cover the rest. Breaking a big task down into these bite-sized tasks makes it less intimidating and more manageable. Once you've done this for each step in your plan, you will end up with something that is clear and easy to follow. With a detailed plan, it is only a matter of time until you reach your goal.

Set a Deadline for Achievement

When you understand what you want to achieve and how much work will go into achieving it, you can figure out how long it might take you to reach your goals. Setting a deadline makes you accountable for getting your work done. Without it, you will procrastinate on getting started. A deadline creates a sense of urgency, encouraging you to get started right away and not waste any more time.

While your deadline should matter, it's okay if things take a bit longer and you end up making adjustments to it later on. It gives you a good goal to shoot for, but unexpected circumstances can get in the way of your initial estimates. If you need to, readjust your time frame as you get a better understanding of how realistic your initial predictions were.

Using the Goal Sheet

Ziglar's goal sheet is an indispensable tool for making progress on your goals. You can use it to organize every step of the goal-planning process. The goal sheet allows you to be more prepared for the challenges you will face, reinforcing your determination, and making you a more effective entrepreneur.

Once you've filled out the goal sheet, pin it somewhere in your office, or wherever you work, so that you can easily refer back to it. If you're ever at a loss for what to do next, look back at your goal sheet and identify your next step. If you're ever feeling unmotivated, remember all of the reasons you are trying to achieve your goals. If you ever find you need a little help, refer back to the list of people and groups who could help you. Keeping the sheet on hand lets you look back at it whenever you need some guidance or motivation so you can get right back to work.

Overall Mindset Approach

The motivational benefit of getting our goals down on paper cannot be understated. It seems like a small step, but writing down our goals really does make us more committed to seeing them through. Our goals go from pleasant daydreams to something we see as achievable, all because we took the time to plan out how we would achieve them. Setting smart goals trains our brains to think of these goals as not just something we want but something we will achieve. Adding a deadline allows us to anticipate the resolution of all of our efforts, which makes it all the easier to get moving on the goals we might have been putting off for months or years.

When we write out a plan, we become much more likely to follow it. We learn exactly how much work our goals will take, and we often find that it is less work than we initially anticipated. When we see that the barrier for success is much lower than we initially assumed, we can get right to work on achieving our life's purposes without hesitation.

Overall Mindset Going Forward

> *"Life is 10% what happens to you and 90% how you react to it"—Charles R. Swindoll*

Your mindset is the foundation of your success. It is what encourages you to start working towards your goals, and it is what will keep you moving no matter what comes next. In your journey to start your own CDL company and accomplish every other long-term goal you set, you are going to face hardships. There are going to be times when you might want to give up. In these moments, the right mindset is the difference between throwing in the towel and finding a way to overcome the challenge. When you believe in your ability to achieve success, and you see everything you can accomplish by moving forward, you will never want to take a step back again.

Becoming CDL-Minded means making the choice to take a proactive role in your own life. It means making the best of any situation and always working towards improving your life, whether it's through establishing and managing your company, or living a fulfilling personal life. Difficulties are inevitable, but how you choose to respond to these difficulties makes all the difference. You can allow the speed bumps and obstacles you encounter to throw you off course. You can adopt a "woe is me" attitude and give up on trying to make your life any better. Or, you can react to whatever life throws at you by maintaining a positive outlook. You can counter misfortune with a can-do attitude and plenty of perseverance. As long as you have a good attitude and a good mindset, there is no difficulty too great for you to overcome.

STEP 2

CDL-Minded in YOUR 'Business'

The 'GAME' Plan for Your Business

The smart goals discussed in the previous chapter work so well because you can use them to create a path for you to follow. Achieving your goals doesn't have to be a guessing game. The way ahead is clear and you know exactly how to proceed because you have created an actionable plan for yourself.

This same method of breaking things down into actionable steps can be used for your business as well. Starting and running a business is a major venture, and it's hard to know exactly where to start and how you're going to expand once you've launched your business. It's critical that you take the time to plan out the steps you will take in a way that is easy to follow and that fits neatly with your vision for your company. To do this, you don't just need a business plan. You need a GAME plan.

What is the GAME Plan?

The GAME plan is an acronym that represents the key components of any good actionable plan for your company. It emphasizes setting specific goals rather than overly general ones that are easy to ignore, as well as making sure your goals are reasonable and measurable. It also encourages you to create a plan that makes you excited to get started right away.

The GAME plan is a deceptively simple formula that produces shockingly powerful results. It is made up of four components. These are making your plan goal-centric, choosing actionable steps, picking goals that are measurable, and setting effective goals and steps toward those goals that you can execute right away.

Goal

We've talked a lot about goal setting so far, but what really is a goal? What makes for a great goal and what makes for a weak one? When you set your goals for your company, what kind of goals should you set?

A great goal is an expectation that you set for yourself. It is something you hold yourself accountable for completing, and something that you believe you will eventually achieve. It is an idea that you envision as part of your future, and ideally it is something that you care deeply about achieving or something that will help you reach other goals you care about. Goals are planned out and acted upon to turn your desires into reality.

When setting company goals, consider all of these factors. Is the goal you set something you actually see yourself achieving, or does it sound impossible? While you can always shoot for the stars, you should try to choose goals that you believe you can accomplish, even if this requires a great deal of hard work. For example, setting a goal of making your company the most successful business in the CDL industry seems motivating at first because you will always work to be the best. However, in practice it can actually be hard to motivate yourself to do this because it is so difficult that your brain tunes it out. You stop holding yourself accountable for it because it feels impossible. A better goal might be to establish a company that generates a profit within the first year, or that makes a certain amount. This goal, while still requiring some work, is definitely achievable, which is a greater incentive for you to complete it.

Actionable

It's all too easy to get advice that isn't specific enough to help. Say your goal was to get in shape and the article you read simply said to start exercising. Exercise should definitely be a part of your plan, but how should you implement it? How long should you exercise for, and what kinds of exercise are best for your specific fitness goals? Without clear, actionable advice, you could make missteps or fail to get started at all because you don't know what's expected of you. If you don't make the plan for achieving your company goals actionable, you could run into the same problem in your business.

An actionable goal is something you can take steps to achieve right now. It is a plan you can realistically put into action as you move forward. It is also one that you have clearly planned out to the extent that you could hand your plan to anyone else, and they could follow it. You want to give yourself specific steps so you don't waste any time wondering what you should do next, and the steps you choose should lead to your goal.

See where you can turn parts of your plan into more actionable steps. If you want to improve the employee training process so new hires know exactly what is expected of them, some actionable steps might be creating a training process that is the same for each employee in a certain job, creating a new employee manual, and writing up step-by-step guides for their first few days on the job. If you want to find more customers, some actionable steps might include creating an online advertising campaign, renting billboard space, or sending out fliers. These goals give you something specific you can do right now to get closer to your long-term goals

Measurable

Another common pitfall when setting goals is failing to make your goals measurable. Setting a measurable goal means you will know exactly when you have achieved it. It is the difference between saying you want to lose some weight and saying you want to lose 10 pounds. You get a clear finish line and you can track your progress toward it every step of the way. Additionally, measurable goals should have a clear deadline. Do you want to lose those 10 pounds in two months or five years? Giving yourself a deadline helps you see if you are making good progress toward achieving your goal on time, or if you need to pick up the pace. Measurable goals are also easier to update once you've achieved them, as you can just increase the numbers and give yourself a new target to shoot for.

Measurable goals are just as important for your business as they are everywhere else. If you decide you want your company to make $10,000 in profit in the first year, you can easily check on your progress every few months and make sure you're still on track to achieve your goal. When you succeed, you can update your goal to $20,000 in profits next year, and keep scaling your goals to match the amount that you want your company to grow.

Effective

Finally, the goals you set should be effective at getting you motivated and encouraging you to take action. You should be able to take the plan you have made and get working on it right away. Even if you cannot do everything on your list on day one, you should at least be able to start with a few tasks and work your way up towards everything else as your company finds its footing.

As you begin to execute your plan, you may find that some steps are more difficult than you initially assumed. It's okay if you have to go back and rework some of your time frames, or you need to break a single step down into smaller ones, in order to accomplish it. If the setback interferes with your motivation, refer back to all of the benefits you will receive as you achieve your goals, and how your company will continue to expand. When you finally reach success, all of the work will have been worth it.

Writing a Company Game Plan

A great company game plan is much more than just a set of steps to follow. It gives your business a real purpose, bringing it closer to your personal mission and vision statement. There is a big difference between a business plan and a real game plan. While a business plan might be used to secure finances or tell others what your company does, your game plan should be primarily written for your own use. It is a way to lay out your goals and projections for the future, making them easier to achieve and also ensuring they line up with your personal goals. Your game plan is to, for, and within your business. It will help guide your decisions and show others what your company is really about, not just how much money it makes.

Of course, money can be part of your game plan too, since it's a part of many goals. One of the greatest benefits of owning a company in the CDL industry is the financial freedom you will enjoy once your company is up and running. Recent estimates say that as a company owner, "you can average about $184,803 per year," not to mention the benefits you'll receive from a recent tax reform plan that pledges "the corporate tax rate will be lowered, a repatriation plan will be in place," and a change to "the way that pass-through business income is taxed" (TanTara, 2019, para. 5-10) in your favor. This all adds up to a very nice paycheck that can help you achieve your other goals as long as you establish and stick to a solid company game plan. Your plan should start with a company ethos that parallels your life's purpose.

Writing a Mission and Vision Statement That Aligns with Your Life's Purpose

If you want to achieve your life's purpose, you need to make the first move. Your company's mission statement should set you up to follow through on your purpose. While there is plenty to look forward to in your future, "it can only be brought into manifestation through desire, faith, or the spoken word" (Shinn, 2005, p. 12). What this means for your company is that while you can achieve great things, opportunities may slip out of your hands if you do not take the proper steps to take advantage of them. You need to put your will out into the universe to get your wishes fulfilled.

Your vision statement is a great way to express your desires to yourself and those around you. It should outline what you want to achieve and why it is so important to get there. Your reasons why should all come from your life's purpose. How does achieving each goal you set for your company bring you closer to your personal and professional goals? How does it help you make an impact on your own life, the lives of your family members, and the lives of those in your community? For example, having a profitable company and plenty of extra money could help you put your kids through college. It could also help you give back to your community or donate money to charitable causes you support. A great mission statement matters to you, as well as your customers, because it shows how your company's success can benefit everyone.

The Importance of Your Business' Mission Statement

We have already discussed how a mission statement can help guide the decisions you make as the leader of your company, and this is still very true. You should try to make decisions that follow through on what you promised in your mission statement, as doing so helps you get closer to achieving your goals. A truly great mission statement, that you hold close to your heart as you make important decisions, also has the hidden advantage of helping out with marketing.

People want to care about your business for reasons other than price or even quality of service. This is the reason why businesses closely tied to charitable causes can often charge a bit more for their services. Customers know that a portion of the profits help to make a positive difference in the world. If customers feel like supporting your business improves their community, or that the money they spend is going to a good cause, they are more likely to choose your company over other options. Hearing a sweet story about how your company is helping kids lead better lives, and the money you make is being used to improve other families' lives, is heartwarming. Wouldn't you want to support a business like that? Having a clear vision and life's purpose for your company encourages brand loyalty and positive word-of-mouth marketing, and great marketing is key to any successful business.

Of all the things you can do for your business, marketing is the most important one. It is absolutely vital for success. Without it, you limit the number of potential customers who see your company and consider choosing it for their needs. If no one knows your company exists, or if you don't have a way to stand out from the crowd of other similar companies, you're going to have a hard time establishing yourself in the CDL market. If you market yourself in a way that helps you really connect with your customers by emphasizing the greater purpose of your company, you will build a loyal base of patrons and attract droves of new customers.

How to Apply Your Mission Statement to Your Business

Once you've come up with a mission statement and purpose for your business, you just need to follow through with it. When you face a difficult decision and you don't know what choice to make, choose the one that aligns closest to your company's vision. When you are trying to expand your company, expand in a way that brings you closer to your company's long-term goals. If you are consistent in your choices, your company will get closer to your vision every day. You will not only create a game plan but also follow through on it.

Registering Your Company as a Cooperative Business or LLC

Now that you've laid the groundwork for your company, it's time to actually establish it. As a small business, you'll want to register your company as a cooperative business (co-op) or a limited liability company (LLC). Doing so offers you greater protections for your personal property, as well as legal and tax advantages. LLCs are a good choice for small businesses. Compared to corporations, they are typically easier to set up, less expensive, and they offer more flexibility.

Registering your business is easier than it sounds. First, you need to appoint a registered agent. The registered agent is the "official point of contact" for the business, and they're required to "sign for and receive legal notices, state mandates, wage garnishments, and tax documents during specific business hours" (Incorporate.com, n.d., para. 7) for the state. You can take this job on yourself or give the responsibility to someone else, but whoever you choose, make sure they will be available when the state calls on them to complete these tasks. If you think you'll be too busy running things, you can appoint a trustworthy business partner instead.

To register as an LLC, you'll also need an employer identification number (EIN). This is used to identify your business and it allows you to open a bank account for your company. You'll also need your EIN for filing taxes. Obtaining an EIN is part of the process of filing your company with the state.

Some, but not all, states require you to create an LLC operating agreement. This is a blueprint for the internal structure of your company. It details who has ownership of the company, the rights of different members, and how profits and losses are distributed, for example. Check with your state and local laws to see if this is a necessary part of your registration process.

Prior to completing these tasks, however, you'll need to decide what kind of LLC you want to register your company as.

Choosing the Right Type of LLC

The type of LLC that's right for your business is largely dependent on the size and structure of your business. There are a few different kinds of LLCs, but you only need to choose between the three most relevant ones for CDL businesses. These are single-member LLCs, general partnerships, and family limited partnerships. The option you choose is based on who you want to have a say, legally, in how your company operates.

As the name implies, single-member LLCs, also known as sole proprietorship businesses, are owned and operated by a single person. You alone would be responsible for any sales your company makes, as well as any taxes and debts the business owes. If you are starting your business with another person or multiple business partners, the general partnership is a better fit for your needs. Each co-owner shares the responsibility for the company's assets and expenses. If you want your business to be a family venture, register as a family limited partnership. With this structure, you can easily transfer control to different members of the family, making it easier to pass down the family business.

Making Your LLC Work for You

The most important benefit that comes with forming an LLC is that it provides protection for you and your assets. When you register your company as an LLC, you separate the company's finances from your own. You still pay yourself from your company's profits, but the resources available to your company and your resources as an individual are treated as two separate entities under the law.

This may not seem like an important distinction, but it can actually make a huge difference in terms of liability. Let's say your business generates debt, or a lawsuit is filed against the company. The liability for paying any associated fees now falls on the company, not you. Debts can only be demanded from your company's bank account and other assets, not your own. This means unless you choose to pay these debts out of your personal bank account, you can't be ordered to pay more than what's in your company's account. You will also avoid having valuable resources like your home or personal car repossessed for a debt incurred by your business. This protection is incredibly valuable for you as a business owner, so forming an LLC is worth the cost and minor hassle of filing the paperwork.

Forming an LLC protects you from a few other liabilities as well. These include liability for your co-owners' actions and your employees' actions if they commit fraud, injure someone, or otherwise act recklessly while they are affiliated with the business. Additionally, if you have personal debts, none of your company's resources can be repossessed to pay these debts without your consent.

Overall Mindset Approach

As the owner of your own company, your actions impact more people than just yourself. You also invite some risk into your life when you start a business. There is every chance that you will find success and wealth with your new company, but there is always a chance, no matter how small, that your company could fail. If you don't take the proper steps to protect yourself from the fallout of significant debt, lawsuits, or bankruptcy, you, your company, and your employees are all at major risk. By forming an LLC, this will allow you to take the necessary steps to protect your assets and look out for your company, and it's a major step you absolutely don't want to skip.

CHAPTER
3

The Secrets to Small Businesses Vs. Large Businesses

The CDL industry is full of businesses, both small and large in scale. Some CDL companies employ fleets of truckers and provide service across the entire nation, while others service a smaller area, such as providing school buses for the schools in a county, or shuttling people to and from work in a certain city. There is a common belief that the bigger your company is, the better, but is this really true? Is it impossible to succeed as a small business, or are there actually some advantages to starting small?

As a small business, it can often feel difficult to compete with larger businesses that may have a greater share of the market than you do. You might feel like you are a small fish in a huge pond full of much bigger fish. You may think that there's no way you can compete with these bigger businesses. The truth is that even though they may have more resources at their disposal, you can still run an incredibly successful small business that is very profitable. In fact, in some ways it is actually better to be a small business because you don't have to deal with many of the difficulties that come with a larger-scale operation. This can give you more control over what you want your company to be and how you will direct its growth.

Learning how to make a small business as profitable as its larger counterparts is a matter of learning to leverage your time in the best way possible. Rather than focusing on trivial matters and small improvements, you need to learn where you can make the biggest improvements to your company by spending the least amount of time. In order to do this, you must also understand what differentiates small businesses from large ones, and how many people have found success running businesses with a more limited scope. If you leverage your time properly, and use the resources you have to your advantage, you can compete with even the largest CDL businesses.

Small and Large Businesses

Just like in any other field, knowing your competition will give you some insight as to how you can find your own place in the market. It's important to understand both the many different kinds of small businesses you might want to create, as well as the differences between these businesses and larger ones. It's also a good idea to get a sense of the similarities that small and large businesses in the CDL industry share. Through this process, you can get an idea of how you can use the unique differences that being a small business provides to your advantage, as well as how you can capitalize on the similarities. Getting a good sense of what the CDL field looks like as a whole, will help you better understand your place in it and assist you in carving out a niche for yourself.

Types of Small CDL Businesses

There are many different kinds of jobs that require a CDL, and there are equally as many types of businesses in the CDL industry. These jobs may involve the transportation of various goods or people across vastly different sized areas. While some jobs are more suited to larger enterprises, such as countrywide delivery along the lines of FedEx and UPS, there are plenty of CDL businesses you can operate on a smaller scale when you are just starting out.

If you don't have much money for start-up costs, there are still some CDL businesses you can run with limited resources. A moving company could be a great place to start, as you just need a large vehicle with storage space, somewhere to park it, and someone to assist with lifting heavy objects. While larger companies like UHaul exist, you can differentiate yourself by providing higher-quality service to a smaller region. Other ideas that are relatively cheap to start include running a small-scale shuttle service for commuters if you live near a big city, or running a tour bus if you're based near a popular destination.

In addition to the previous two options, there are many types of CDL companies that are influenced by where you live. For example, if you live near a lake or ocean you might operate a boat towing service. If there is an airport nearby, you might make your money with a company that shuttles people to and from their planes, especially if the airport is underserved by taxis. You might even look into transporting livestock if you live somewhere more rural.

Many CDL companies work alongside other industries. Waste hauling, water hauling, and septic hauling are all examples of this symbiotic relationship. Furniture delivery is another option if you are interested in contracting with stores that aren't big enough to offer their own service. You might start a similar business that helps haul large appliances to and from peoples' homes. Hauling large, bulky construction equipment is another viable option, as well as starting a towing company, provided you get the right permits for each.

No matter where your interests lie or where you live, there are plenty of ways to start working in the CDL industry even if you don't yet have the money to buy a whole fleet of trucks or shuttles. Choose a type of business that is interesting to you, and that helps bring you closer to achieving your goals without sacrificing the things that matter most.

Differences Between Running Small and Large Businesses

There are many differences between small and large businesses, especially at the company ownership level. While large businesses may have the capability to generate more money, there are also plenty of problems unique to these large companies. Running a large business means keeping track of hundreds or even thousands of different clients, not to mention just as many employees. It means business owners either spreading themselves thin or delegating tasks to others who may or may not complete them to their approval. People who own large businesses may need to spend more time at work just to manage everything at their companies, which means less free time to spend with friends and family. While there may be more cash flow, there is less opportunity to enjoy the benefits of owning their own business.

When you have a small business, many of these growing pains disappear because there is a lot less for you to keep track of. You will likely only manage a handful of other employees, and if you need to delegate any work, you can choose someone you trust to take over the responsibility. You have more control over your business and how daily operations are run. You also have greater control over your life as a whole as there are fewer demands on your time. While you may still look to expand your small business, operating at a small scale isn't always a bad thing.

Small businesses also get to enjoy the benefits of being classified as an LLC, which is much less complex than registering a huge company. While you will still have to pay some LLC registration fees, these fees are much cheaper than what larger companies pay. You also don't have to worry about nearly the same risk of liability, which gives you a little more freedom for how you want your company to operate.

Similarities Between Running Small and Large Businesses

Though there are plenty of differences, small and large businesses in the CDL industry have some things in common as well. Running either type of business can provide you with a sizable income that opens many future paths for you. A CDL business of any size can help you break out of a routine job that leaves you exhausted for an average paycheck. You can achieve a startling level of success in the commercial driving industry, whether you run and maintain a small company, or you work your way up to a large fleet of drivers that service many different customers.

The main thing that small and large businesses have in common is the need for passion and a good mindset. At the end of the day, small or large, these are all companies in the same industry. Genuine appreciation for CDL jobs ties the industry together, and the best leaders in businesses of all sizes have adopted the CDL-Minded approach. If you have a goal-oriented state of mind and you really care about your business, you will fit right in no matter the size of your company.

How to Utilize These Resources to Your Advantage

As a small business, you're not going to have access to the same number of resources that bigger companies get. You may not have very many employees, and as a result you may be limited in the number of customers you can take on at the beginning. Part of expanding your business is learning to work with the resources you have and maximize your profits, even in a small-scale company.

Owning a small business doesn't mean you can't succeed. It just means that you have to be smarter about using the resources at your disposal. You may not have access to a fleet of hundreds of trucks, but you can buy a few trucks, and ensure that the drivers for each truck are providing the highest quality of service. You may not have many people working under you that can manage whole sections of your company for you, but this just means that you get more direct control over every part of your business. As a small company, you can shape your company so it best fits the purpose you outlined in your mission statement.

CDL-Minded Approach

In commercial driving companies, success can be found in a wide variety of businesses. The typical image that CDL brings to mind, of driving a truck all across the country, is a viable option, but it's far from the only one. Because of this, anyone in the CDL industry can succeed, no matter how much money you have when you founded your company. You can start with a small operation of just a handful of people, and slowly grow it over time into a business that makes well over $100,000 a year. Both small and large businesses can find success, so long as you make proper use of your resources.

One of the most important resources to learn how to manage is time. If you want to achieve great success, learn to leverage your time to best suit your needs. Many people believe that it's better to spend time to save money, but it's actually better and effective to spend money to save yourself some time. While saving time can help you make your money back, saving money can't rewind the clock. When you use your time effectively you will see an amazing return on your investments, no matter how large your business is.

The Art of Leveraging Time

The common misconception of time is that "time is the most valuable resource." While time is certainly an important resource, it isn't nearly as valuable as energy. Your energy impacts everything you do, from how much work you can get done in a day to how much passion you have for your business. Without energy, you could have all the time in the world and still not get anything done. It can even help you manage your time well and use it efficiently, which allows you to properly leverage your time. How you use your energy and time will determine how valuable your resources are and how successful you can be.

When you leverage your time well, you apply your energy to the areas that need it most. This helps you focus on what matters, and you get the greatest effect for the least amount of time spent. You only have so much energy every day. Overworking yourself and ending up exhausted doesn't do your productivity any favors. It's better to use your time and energy wisely and work on the most important things first, while you still have the energy to get them done. In order to do this, you need to identify the areas with the greatest potential for growth in your business.

One of the biggest obstacles to leveraging your time effectively is focusing on the wrong things. If you let the small stuff get in the way, you could end up wasting all of your time and energy on something that is only going to provide a little bit of growth for your company. For example, say you put a lot of energy into improving your negotiation skills. You read books about charisma and making deals, you attend seminars, and you get plenty of practice negotiating. This might let you negotiate slightly better contracts, but how much does that help you in the long run? Is it better to make a few extra dollars from a handful of contracts, or would it be better to attract many new customers and double the number of contracts your company has? The latter option has a much higher growth potential and it will make you more money for less effort.

In proper time management, you want to look at the things that are going to have the biggest impact on your success. Keep the big picture in mind and always look for ways that you can get closer to your long-term goals; don't get bogged down by short-term solutions. Instead of putting all your energy into negotiation skills, it might be a better investment of your time and energy to focus on marketing so you can reach more customers. You can make more money than you ever could from making tiny improvements to the terms of each contract. From there, you'll build a more long-lasting business, if you expand your customer base. While negotiation is still a good skill to have under your belt, pursue it only if it will make the biggest impact on your business. Looking at the long-term effects of how you spend your time will help you make the right calls.

How to Effectively Leverage Your Time

Effective time management requires you to be able to set priorities for your tasks. You want to work on the important things first, and save everything else for later, or you risk wasting energy on things that are less important. If you have a lot of work to get done, consider what will bring you the greatest gain by finishing it, and what will have the greatest consequences if you don't get it done by the end of the day. Work on these tasks first, even and especially if they are the hardest tasks. You have the most energy right at the beginning of the day, so use it in the best possible way and make the best use of your time.

Delegation is another key component of good time management. For every task, consider who would be best suited for the job. This could be you, or it could be someone else in your company. Learning to identify "the skills, knowledge and abilities you possess and spending your time leveraging these talents will provide you with the most productive and profitable impact" (Gatty, 2017, para. 2). Know what you're good at and know what others are good at, and assign each task to the person who will do the best job. If you're not strong with finances, delegate the task to someone who is, or hire someone for the job. If you're great at employee oversight, focus on that, and leave routine paperwork and answering the phones to someone else. When done correctly, delegation keeps you from wasting time on tasks you aren't great at and lets you spend your energy where it is most needed.

While you want your company to operate efficiently, you should prioritize effectiveness. Efficiency means you are completing tasks as quickly as possible. While this is good, it doesn't always allow for you to determine if the tasks you're doing are actually worth doing. You don't want to just fill your schedule. You want to focus on the tasks that actually matter and cut out busy work wherever you can in order to make your business more effective. Consider whether lengthy processes need to be done at all or if there's a better alternative. Figure out if you can train others to do tasks and free up your own time to focus on big-picture activities. Look for alternatives to spending excessive time and energy on tasks. All of this ensures that your business is operating as effectively as possible.

The Overall Mindset Approach

The idea of running a small business can feel very limiting. You may initially feel that there's no way you can compete with bigger businesses, and you may have concerns about getting pushed out of the market. However, with energy management skills and a goal-oriented mindset, you can still run a highly successful and competitive company.

When you really consider the advantages and disadvantages of running a small business compared to a larger one, you will start to see that, if you manage your resources right, a small business can still help you achieve success. Learning to leverage your time effectively helps you make the best use of your resources, even if you have access to fewer resources than large companies. If you work to become the best company you can be at your current scale, you can expand your business over time or just maximize your effectiveness as a small business. Either way, you will have plenty of opportunities to keep working towards your life's purpose.

CHAPTER 4

Expenses You MUST KNOW in Your CDL Business

As much as running a CDL business can be a labor of love, at the end of the day it is also a company that needs to remain profitable in order to continue operating. If you want to run a successful business, you need to consider the financial aspect, and that means accounting for all of the expenses your company will generate. If you want to turn a profit, you need to know how much money you're going to spend just to get things running.

The type and scale of your business will have an impact on how much it costs to operate. Larger businesses generally cost more, though they can bring in more money as well. Smaller businesses are usually much cheaper to run, but the expenses they do have are still important to consider. Different kinds of CDL businesses will cost different amounts as well. It might be cheaper to run a small tour bus company that only requires two or three buses and a small staff, than it is to run a delivery company where more drivers and more trucks are needed. Still, as long as you account for the expenses in your industry, you can make enough money that these costs aren't a problem. If you make smart financial decisions that account for common sources of debt in the CDL industry, you can keep your business highly profitable.

Common Expenses in the CDL Industry

While the details of the expenses that each company has to worry about are a little different, there are some common expenses that are present in almost all CDL businesses, no matter the service they provide or their size. Knowing what these expenses are and how much they can cost, you can better prepare you to make a financial plan that helps you offset these costs. Consider how each of these expenses might affect your own business.

Vehicles

All CDL businesses have vehicle expenses. Whether your business uses trucks, vans, buses, shuttles, or any other type of commercial vehicle, buying the vehicle is one of the first big purchases you will make. If you need many vehicles to run your business, the costs can add up quickly. While these are one-time purchases, you also need to worry about maintenance costs, which become more frequent the longer it's been since you bought the vehicles. Don't forget about insurance too, including physical damage, bobtail insurance for trucks without trailers, and occupational accident insurance. While you might be tempted to go with cheaper insurance plans, this could result in a higher bill if an accident does occur.

Vehicle purchase and maintenance expenses are unavoidable, but good preparation will ensure these costs aren't a problem for you. Make budget estimates for new vehicles and maintenance, and set money aside for these expenses long before they appear. This way, you can deal with engine issues or flat tires quickly and without stress, helping your drivers get back on the road as soon as possible and minimizing delays.

Fuel

If you're driving thousands of miles, you're going to need to pay for thousands of miles of fuel. Unfortunately, fuel isn't cheap, so this can very quickly turn into tens of thousands of dollars of expenses. Fuel costs are less of a concern for businesses that service a local area, but they're still something you should keep in mind, no matter how far your vehicles drive on a daily basis.

If you have a good idea of how many miles you're going to cover, you can use this information to figure out how much money you should set aside for fuel costs. Take the miles per gallon of your vehicle and divide it by the cost of fuel per gallon, then multiply the result by your estimated mileage in a given length of time, and you will get an estimate of just how much you will spend on gas for the same length of time. If your business involves multiple trucks, make sure to account for all of them. Neglecting to consider fuel costs is a quick way to bankrupt yourself, but as long as you save enough money, you should be making enough in revenue to offset these costs.

Employee Wages

If your business employs other people, you'll need to make sure you account for their salaries in your expense estimates. Employee wages will hit your wallet harder as your business grows larger, but they shouldn't be ignored in smaller businesses either. Short of laying off employees or severely cutting workers' pay, there isn't too much you can do to minimize these expenses either. It helps to make sure you are only hiring the number of people that you need to do the amount of work you have. If business is slow, you may need fewer employees than you initially anticipated until things pick up, but don't under staff yourself either. If your business is seasonal, consider hiring employees on a seasonal basis as well.

Registering Your Company

Earlier, we talked about the importance of registering your company as an LLC. While the benefits are well worth the price, forming an LLC is still an expense you should account for when you're budgeting. You'll need to pay a state filing fee, the cost of which can vary by the state. If you completed the LLC process through a company with the help of an expert, you'll have to pay their fees as well. On top of this, you'll be expected to pay annual fees to keep your LLC current and valid. For the most part, these are unavoidable fees, but don't forget about them when you're calculating your expenses.

Taxes

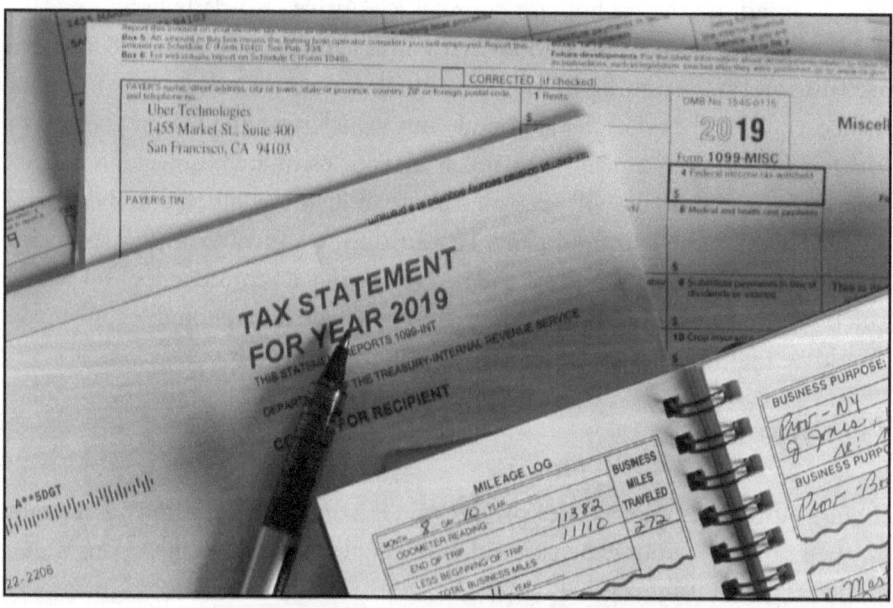

Taxes are a significant expense for any business, and CDL businesses are just as heavily affected by them as any other. Whether you're running a business or having them taken out of every paycheck, "Taxes are your largest single expense" (Wheelwright, 2018, p. 20). Taxes take a cut of your business' profits, which can leave you with less money than you initially anticipated. However, while taxes are dreaded by just about everyone, do they really have to be so bad?

If you understand tax laws and follow the right steps, you can minimize the amount of money you pay out in taxes. When you make proper use of all available tax breaks, you can save yourself a lot of money, and a lot of stress too. We will discuss the specifics of lowering the amount you pay in taxes shortly, but for now, it is enough to know that no matter how much you end up paying, taxes should be factored into your expenses.

How to Maintain a Consistent Cash Flow

With so many expenses that could cost you thousands of dollars, you need to make sure you're generating and saving enough money to cover all of the costs that come with a CDL business. Part of this process is finding customers and making money from jobs, but another part is learning how to properly manage the money you make. If you spend the revenue from your first few jobs immediately, you're going to be completely caught off-guard when the bills come in, and you don't have any money saved up to pay them off. Without consistent cash flow and proper savings, the harsh truth is that your business won't last long. You need to keep your expenses low and keep your income high, as well as get into the habit of saving before spending.

Start Marketing

Marketing is the best way to find potential customers for your business. When you market yourself, you show others how your company does business and why they should choose you over your competitors. More customers means more revenue coming into your business, which can help to offset many of the costs generated from running a business. While marketing can add to your expenses at first, it is typically fairly cheap compared to the amount you'll be spending on trucks and fuel, and a great marketing strategy will more than make up for the amount you spend on it.

As your company services more customers, you're going to increase in size. This means your expenses will increase as well. To balance your income and spending, you'll want to have a solid, reliable financial plan that guides your purchasing habits and cuts down on wasteful spending.

Create a Financial Plan for Your Business

Your financial plan outlines all of the steps you need to take to become a profitable business and continue expanding your sales. Most contain multiple different components such as your sales forecast, your expenses budget, a statement of your current financial position, your cash flow projection, and an operations plan that explains your specific goals and how you plan to achieve them. Just like starting a business without long-term goals, trying to grow financially without a plan can leave you struggling to figure out what comes next and what you want to achieve. In a study of small business owners, results showed that "entrepreneurs who had a completed business plan for their venture were more than twice as likely to successfully grow their business as those who had no plan or an incomplete financial plan" (Wertz, n.d., para. 2). If you want to double your chances of success, a complete financial plan is mandatory.

Begin with your sales forecast. This is an estimate of the revenue you will make from your sales. Try to make estimates on a monthly, quarterly, and yearly basis to paint a more complete picture. If you have previous sales, look back at these for your estimates and pay attention to any patterns that might arise—for example, certain types of businesses might do better seasonally or during certain kinds of weather. If you haven't been operating for a few months already, make a good estimate based on how many customers you have and how much you charge for your service. Getting a good idea of your current sales will help you figure out how much you want to grow your sales in the future.

Next, make a budget of all of your company expenses. We have already discussed the most common ones for CDL businesses, but include any others that are relevant to your company. Make sure you write down current operation costs and expected expenses you will have in the future. For example, if you want to grow your business, plan on spending more on the necessary expenses. You may also need to budget for wage increases or tax rate increases, as well as setting some money aside for unexpected expenses like damage to your business caused by fires or natural disasters. It's better to save money for these costs even if they don't happen than to be caught by surprise if they do happen.

Your statement of your current financial position should list your assets and your liabilities. Account for all of your assets, like machinery, inventory, and property, and make sure you include all of your outstanding bills. This step gives you an idea of where you are right now. If your assets outweigh your liabilities, you're on the right track. If your liabilities are much higher, you may need to see where you can cut some costs and pay off some of your bills.

The cash flow projection is similar to your sales forecast, but it looks at how much you will have left on a monthly, quarterly, and yearly basis. It is your income minus your expenses for a given period of time. If you have cash left at the end of each period, you can put that money to good use such as expanding or investing in your business. If you're short on cash, making a cash flow projection helps you notice this issue before it can build into extreme debt.

Now that you understand where you currently are, you can start looking towards the future with your operations plan. This overview will help you understand "what roles are required to operate your business at various volumes of output, how much output or work each employee can handle, and the costs of each stage of your supply chain" (Wertz, n.d., para. 25). A good operations plan will help you identify where there is room to grow and how you should make financial decisions in the future. Give yourself clear, measurable goals to work towards in the future, like increasing revenue 10% or lowering expenses by $5,000.

Make Your Taxes Work for You

Taxes are a large part of your operating expenses, but they don't have to be overwhelming. There are many ways to get your taxes to work for you. The process involves taking advantage of tax breaks available for your business, thereby minimizing the amount you are required to pay.

As a small business owner, there are many tax breaks available to you that don't require you to take advantage of loopholes. In fact, the government actually wants you to take advantage of these tax breaks. As professional CPA Thomas Wheelwright notes in his book *Tax-Free Wealth: How to Build Massive Wealth by Permanently Lowering Your Taxes*, tax codes are written "as government incentives and economic stimulus to keep the wheels of the economy greased and moving," (Wheelwright, 2018, p. 8) so you're doing exactly what the government wants by making the most of every tax break you can.

Here are some tax deductions that may apply to your business:

- Gas
- Travel expenses that are covered by the company
- Office supplies
- Vehicle maintenance costs like new tires, parts, and other repairs
- CDL licensing fees
- CDL education classes
- Mileage deductions
- Business and renter's insurance
- Startup expenses
- Employee salaries and benefits
- Home office expenses
- Phone and internet
- Loan interest
- Legal, bookkeeping, and accounting service fees
- Depreciation of vehicles
- Charity donations

Avoid Legal Fines

It's also important to make sure your business is compliant with all relevant laws and codes. Neglecting to do so could leave you with a hefty fine.

Important areas to pay attention to are licensing, zoning, environmental laws, city ordinances, and safety.

For licensing requirements, make sure you and your employees all have the proper CDL credentials for the job. You may also need to get one or more endorsements if you're working in specific areas like passenger transport or hazardous waste transport. Check the licensing laws in your state as well as federal laws for transporting goods and people across state lines.

Zoning laws can throw a real wrench in your business if you don't check them before you begin operating. Some states have restrictions on where you can and can't start certain types of businesses. You may need to move your business elsewhere if you live somewhere that doesn't allow for business operations or for the large trucks or buses that your CDL company uses.

As a company with the potential to increase greenhouse gas emissions, you will be subject to many environmental health laws created by the Environmental Protection Agency (EPA). These laws ensure that transportation companies are operating in a way that reduces their carbon footprint. While you may have to work to abide by these policies in your business, you can get some tax breaks for following them too. For example, as part of the Clean Diesel Program, "The EPA offers grants and rebates for projects that improve air quality by reducing harmful emissions from diesel engines" (Entrepreneur, 2016, para. 23). Making use of these rebates can help you lower your expenses.

Your town or city may have specific ordinances that your business needs to follow. These ordinances may be about hours of operation or other guidelines for all businesses in the area, or there may be specific ordinances for your CDL business. Check local laws and keep up with any new ordinances passed to ensure you are in compliance with them.

Finally, you should ensure that your business is operating as safely as possible. While there is always a chance for accidents to occur, you should be doing everything in your power to reduce that chance. Big accidents could leave people seriously hurt, not to mention the fines and bad press you would get. Managing safety concerns in your business will be addressed in greater detail in a future chapter.

Make Use of People, Tools, and Other Resources That Can Help

There are plenty of tools that can help you manage your company's financial plan. It's a good idea to invest in an accounting software or a budgeting program so you can keep all of your financial information in one place. These programs can help you stay on track and hit your profit targets by highlighting any areas where your spending is exceeding your income.

If you find that you need more help than that, you may want to hire someone to help you manage your finances. While you should always be in charge of the direction you want to take your business, it's not a bad idea to hire an accountant who is responsible for the details of your expenses. Accountants can break all of your financial information down into something that's easier to understand, letting you make informed decisions for your company. Accountants can also help manage your taxes and identify where you can make use of tax breaks. While hiring or contracting an accountant may cost you some money, you typically make much more back by following their advice, so it's a good investment for your business as you continue to grow.

Take a CDL-Minded Approach to Your Expenses

The financial side of any business can be overwhelming, but if you treat it the same way you treat your other goals, it becomes an easier issue to manage. Consider what you want to achieve, then break it down into smaller steps to get there. If you want to increase your revenue, find new customers through marketing or increase your rates. If you want to improve your profit-to-expenses ratio, find ways you can cut out unnecessary spending. Set financial goals that will help you grow your company and assist you in achieving your other long-term goals.

CHAPTER 5

The Road to Obtaining Unlimited Freedom

Running your own company has its perks, and many of those perks come in the form of greater professional and personal freedom. After all, becoming an entrepreneur isn't a job for everyone. If you're okay sitting at a desk working a nine-to-five every day, pulling long hours, and trying to manage a limited number of sick days, then you wouldn't be so interested in starting and running a CDL business. You most likely wanted a little more control in your life and some more flexibility in your schedule. In short, you wanted to experience unlimited freedom. But what does unlimited freedom really look like, and how will starting your own CDL business help you experience it?

In the CDL industry, freedom comes in many forms. Even truck drivers who are employed by CDL companies can generally experience more freedom in their jobs than people who have corporate positions. There is no rigid structure in a trucking job. Drivers get to experience the freedom of the open road, and where they stop, eat, and sleep is largely at their own discretion. What supervision does exist is limited, as drivers are often hundreds of miles away from their supervisors. Additionally, commercial driving is a lucrative industry, and even the drivers experience greater financial freedom than what's offered at many other companies. However, there are still some limitations to this kind of freedom. Truck drivers may have to spend time away from home, and working long shifts is often just part of the job. This could mean less time spent with family. If you want to experience real, unlimited freedom, running your own company where you call the shots, gives you the most control over your own life and how you want to live it.

What unlimited freedom means to you, as a CDL-Minded Entrepreneur, is having the freedom to live as you see fit and the control and shape your life in the direction you want. You can work at your own discretion and create a business that reflects your own values and principles. You won't have anyone standing over your shoulder as you work criticizing your efforts, because you're the boss. A successful business means you can even spend freely, no longer tied down by extensive budgeting just to be able to afford the basics. There will be obstacles in your path as you expand your business, but when you overcome them, you will experience freedom like you've never known it before.

How to Achieve Freedom

The good news is that you're already on the right path to achieving freedom. You've made the commitment to owning your own CDL business, which will help you find freedom in your career that carries over to your personal life. Part of developing more control over your life is expanding your business and striving towards your goals, which is what you have been learning to do this whole time.

The not-so-good news is that you will still face some roadblocks on your way to freedom. Ironically, some of these obstacles come from freedom itself. After all, if you're not used to having control over your schedule, you might be more tempted to procrastinate important work. Without a clear path ahead of you, you might not know where to go. These kinds of obstacles are especially harmful because they don't seem like problems at first, which means you might not address bad habits until they've become ingrained in your schedule. You can overcome these obstacles, but only if you learn to recognize them.

Obstacles to Achieving Freedom

Too much freedom, too quickly, can leave us scrambling to readjust. The "freedom adjustment" here is so great because we have never experienced so much freedom before, which can leave us uncertain how to handle it (G-Town, n.d., para. 4). Think of a kid going to college for the first time and using their newfound independence away from home to cut class and attend parties, but with even fewer restrictions. If you can't adjust to the amount of responsibility you need to take for your own actions, you won't get important work done and the company will suffer.

Financial issues and debt are also obstacles to achieving freedom. One way to protect yourself from its effects is to register as an LLC. This ensures you're not going to be held personally responsible for any debts or legal trouble your company faces, which might otherwise compromise your financial freedom.

By far the biggest obstacle to your freedom, more than any financial hiccups your company may experience or competition you may face, is your own mindset. The danger of the freedom adjustment exemplifies how you can get in your own way even when the road ahead should be clear. If you can continue focusing on your goals and maintaining self-discipline even when the only thing keeping you from straying from the path is yourself, you can safely make the adjustment to unlimited freedom.

How to Apply Unlimited Freedom

As you adjust to the new levels of freedom you experience as a CDL entrepreneur, you may be left uncertain as to how you can manage your excess time, money, and control over your life. This freedom is everything you've been working toward, but what will you do with it now that you have it?

As always, whenever you feel directionless or lost, return to your goals. These will point you in the right direction. Consider what goals you've set for the future of your business. Have you achieved all of these, or can you keep working towards them? Are there ways that you can continue to grow your business, or are there other life goals that you can focus on now that you have a better financial situation? Consider the family and community goals you set and keep shaping your life as you see fit. Set new goals that bring you closer to achieving your life's purpose, whatever it may be.

Make sure to push away the desire to procrastinate now that you're free to do what you want. While it's okay to spend some time on celebrating the goals you've achieved, you don't want to get complacent and give up on the rest of your long-term goals. Use the momentum from establishing your business and get everything running by looking for ways to keep growing and expanding your business. This will keep you motivated and reduce the risk of putting off your goals.

How to Get Your Business Working for You

As you continue to grow your business, you may find that you don't need to be quite as directly involved as you did when you were just entering the industry. Hiring more employees means there are more people to take on the jobs you previously had to handle on your own. Outlining your goals and your plan to achieve these goals means you can just follow the steps you have already laid out for yourself. As you delegate tasks to others who become more confident and experienced in their roles over time, you won't need to work for your business—your business will start working for you, affording you much more free time and greater freedom overall.

You can continue to make money even while letting your company effectively run itself, by creating a good foundation and supervising your business' growth. With the right investments, your company will begin generating income like a well-oiled machine, all without you having to spend long nights at work and away from your family. The key to this lies in the three POIs and the three PORs of running your business. We will break these abbreviations down further shortly so you can see how each one applies to your business. They will allow you to take a more hands-off approach to your business, though you will still be the one responsible for guiding the direction of your company's growth and making all the big decisions.

The Overall Mindset Approach

While freedom is desirable, a great deal of freedom all at once can be hard to handle, especially if you're used to heavily structured jobs. If you maintain a good mindset and you don't lose focus, you can keep working towards bigger and better things. It's easy to get distracted by how much freedom you have, or to let concerns fall by the wayside. Resist the temptation and keep up the good work in all areas of your life. If you can continue to motivate yourself using your long-term goals and the lifestyle habits of routines, discipline, and focus, you can use your newfound freedom to achieve even more in life.

The Three POIs You MUST Know in Business

There are three different POIs you need to know in business. Each of these abbreviations will help you keep your business running profitably and allow you to generate cash flow with minimal effort. Putting them to good use can drastically improve your business' revenue, helping you build a business that works for you.

The three POIs are profit of investing, power of input, and producing ongoing income.

Profit of Investing

A great investment will pay out in dividends. When you invest, you give a little bit of your money, time, or other resources, and in exchange, you get an incredible return on your investment. A smart investment is always worth the initial cost. Just as you might invest in stocks, you can also invest in yourself and your company, with more reliable and predictable results than most stock traders enjoy. Through the profit of investing, you can make a small sacrifice work to your advantage.

The Law of Sacrifice was popularized by public speaker and life coach Bob Proctor, who identified it as "giving up something of a lower nature to receive something of a higher nature" (Proctor, 2011). It doesn't mean giving up important things like your health or massive amounts of money. Instead, it means letting go of something small to get something much better in return. Rather than being the painful experience you might associate with the word sacrifice, this law helps you achieve much more than you had before. This law shows us how working hard to overcome adversity can pay off for us, if we invest our time and energy appropriately.

Proper sacrifice is all about self-discipline. It is understanding that a little hardship now is worth the results you will see later. Your efforts are a small price to pay for the rewards you will reap. While investments are most commonly associated with finances, money isn't the only thing you can invest. You can also invest your time and energy to see really amazing results.

The most important places to make investments in are yourself, your family and your business. Investing in yourself involves cultivating skills like the lifestyle habits of discipline and focus. It means learning more about your business and understanding how you can continue to grow as a person and as a leader. Just by reading this book, you are investing in your future success. Investing in your business might involve paying for marketing campaigns to generate more business, hiring accountants for better financial health, or getting more trucks and drivers so you can keep up with demand. All these investments increase the future health of your business. Even if you have to pay a little money or spend more time outlining goals and plans now, the future success will more than make up for it.

Invest in people, tools, and other resources for your business as well. Offer training to your employees, so they can do their jobs more effectively. Invest in more expensive but higher quality vehicles to reduce the risk of drivers breaking down on the side of the road, which can lead to huge delays. When you work on improving what matters most, you will set yourself up to continue to succeed.

Power of Input

What you put into your business is what you get out of it. If you don't get the ball rolling, you'll never start your business at all. If you establish your business but you don't encourage its continued growth, you're not going to see the same results as someone who is constantly looking for ways to improve their business. The power of input highlights just how important it is to put in work so you can reap the rewards of that work later on.

Of course, it's also important to remember that not all ideas are necessarily good ones. If you try to expand your business too rapidly, you could end up bankrupting yourself from all the expenses before you ever get a chance to make back your money. Bad ideas can be just as dangerous as having no ideas for growth at all. It is up to you to evaluate ideas before you apply them in your business.

As the owner of your CDL business, your input and your ability to evaluate others' input is critical to your company's well-being. You may have many employees and advisors, but at the end of the day, it should be your vision that guides the company. If an idea doesn't align with your company's mission statement and it doesn't help you achieve your life's purpose, it may not be a good idea to incorporate it into your business plan. Carefully evaluate each decision and make sure it is the right one for your company.

When you get good input, act on it. Great advice is only useful if you actually put it into action. While you should take time to seriously consider big decisions, don't wait so long that the input is useless. Put your objectives and plans into action by embracing the new strategy.

Just like many other aspects of your business, the power of input starts with your mindset. Your long-term goals will play a large role in helping you decide what paths to follow and what advice could spell trouble for your company. If you are committed to growing your company and seeing your vision fulfilled, it will be much easier to put good input into practice.

Providing Ongoing Income

Your investments and good judgment allow your business to maintain a healthy cash flow. Your company can provide ongoing passive income, which is revenue that is acquired without direct work and accumulates on its own. It will continue to generate this passive income, and all you have to do to ensure continued cash flow is keep providing guidance. This is the stage where your earlier investments pay off.

There are many ways that you can increase the amount of ongoing income generated by your business. Most of these methods focus on increasing the number of customers your business serves, as this will allow you to continually increase your income without additional work on your part. Networking and looking for opportunities to collaborate with other businesses and business leaders can help you expand your customer base. So can making an effort to attend events related to your industry. Marketing is great for attracting new customers and increasing your revenue. You might also encourage your employees to follow up with leads and upsell current clients to make sure you're making as much money as possible out of each job. These are little ways to make a big difference in your ongoing income.

Making financial investments in stocks with your revenue is another way to generate passive interest. If you want to do this, it's a good idea to enlist the help of a trained professional, like a broker, to help you make good decisions, especially if you've never tried to invest before. You can make interest on your investment, and you can be paid dividends just by owning shares in certain companies. If your investment increases in value, the resulting income is known as capital gains. Investing can allow you to take advantage of certain tax breaks too. For example, "Passive income can be written off with passive losses, which are usually expenses associated with operating the income-generating activities" (Cussen, 2020, para. 22). These kinds of tax breaks will save you a lot of money, so they're worth the investment.

As you continue to grow your company, the amount of work you have to do will decrease over time. Your investments will generate their own income, and you won't have to spend all your time operating the minute details of the company. Your money works for you, not the other way around. This gives you the freedom to spend your time pursuing your other life goals.

Mastering the Three POIs for Power, Security, and Freedom

Learning and implementing the three POIs in how you run your business will bring you major financial success. These skills are crucial, and making good use of them will bring you closer to your long-term goals.

Each of the POIs can give you greater power over your life, greater security in your investments, and greater freedom overall. The profit of investing shows you how you can achieve more with your company through initial sacrifice that leads to future success. When you start investing, whether you invest in your own company or you invest your money in stocks, you will benefit greatly at the expense of only a relatively minor setback or financial contribution. These investments are worth what you get back.

You can further increase your chances of making good investments when you exercise good judgment with the power of input. The power of input helps you control where your company is headed so you can profit from its continued success. When all of the POIs are used together, financial concerns and wasted time and energy will be a thing of the past. With these key strategies, unlimited freedom is within your grasp, especially when you combine them with the three PORs.

The Three PORs You MUST Know in Business

The three PORs are all about setting goals for your company and maintaining a goal-oriented mindset. These abbreviations keep your focus on making future plans for your business that will help it continue to succeed. They emphasize the importance of being CDL-Minded and leveraging your time properly, choosing to spend your energy on the tasks that will actually help you achieve your goals. Through proper prioritization, you can ensure that you're not wasting energy on tasks that won't make a big difference on your level of success.

The three PORs are the power of reset, the profit of return, and the plan of reorganization.

Power of Reset

The power of reset is about rest and regeneration. When you are focused on your goals, it's easy to lose yourself in your work. You don't want to exhaust yourself, as this can lead to lower quality work. Taking a moment to reset your thoughts can help you refocus on what you need to be doing.

However, this rest is not idle. Instead of just taking a vacation day and relaxing on a beach, you should aim to calm your thoughts so you can achieve greater concentration. Your goals should be at the forefront of your thoughts as you mentally reset yourself. Through the power of reset, you will regenerate, not just your mindset now, but also your goals and plans for the future.

Focus can come from many different sources, and what you find helpful might be different from what someone else uses to reset. A little bit of exercise can get your blood pumping and clear your head. Try going on a light walk when you feel yourself getting frustrated or overwhelmed, or do a couple of jumping jacks in your office. You might feel a little silly, but the results are worth the temporary embarrassment. Other great strategies include breathing exercises and meditation. These help clear your mind of stressful thoughts, allowing you to center yourself and focus on what really matters. Meditate on your goals and visualize what achieving them might feel like. This can give you the motivation and clarity of thought to start working productively again.

It's best to avoid rest activities like watching TV or playing video games in the middle of work. Instead of helping you achieve greater focus, these kinds of activities pull your attention elsewhere. They're perfectly fine things to do when you're relaxing after work, but they're better left at home if you want to make real progress towards your goals.

Profit of Return

The profit of return is a strategy for executing plans or tasks that will actually generate interest for yourself. It means not wasting your time on the small stuff that doesn't have a big enough impact on the health of your business. It is closely related to learning how to leverage your time to achieve the greatest results. You can remain busy all day, but if the tasks you're doing don't matter, you won't get any of the important work done. Avoid doing work that doesn't need your attention and focus on the things that are going to have a real, measurable impact on your company. Using your time and energy strategically will enable you to get much more work done each day.

To better understand which actions are valuable and which ones aren't, consider the return on investment (ROI) of each of the actions you take. Your ROI is a measure of how much gain you get from doing a certain task. To calculate the ROI, compare your initial investment in time or money to the results of what you invested. For example, say you make phone calls to your customers and renegotiate your contracts. You make 10% more revenue in contracts than you otherwise would have made that day, so if you typically generated $1,000 in a day you would have made $1,100. Your ROI is the extra 10% gain, or $100 you made that day. Was this really a productive use of your time? Could you have done other tasks that would have brought in far more than an extra $100? If so, then you need to consider how to maximize your energy efficiency by doing tasks that have a bigger impact on your business' success.

To improve your ROI, consider how you could either complete these tasks more efficiently or let someone else handle them. Instead, you might choose to write out a single email and send it out to all of your previous customers, cutting down on the time investment, or you might delegate the task to someone else, as it doesn't require much expertise to do.

Delegation is a key skill for business owners to learn. Consider what each member of your team is best at and see if they would be a good fit for any of the tasks on your plate. This doesn't mean handing over anything you don't want to do; instead, it means analyzing your staff's strengths and weaknesses, and giving them the work they can complete more efficiently than anyone else.

Pass down tasks that take a lot of time and don't provide a great deal of value to your business. While these tasks may be necessary, they don't necessarily have to get done by you. For example, cleaning the bathrooms in the office is a necessary task that has to get done, but it would be unusual, to say the least, if you spent your energy scrubbing toilets instead of making important decisions for your business. Treat these busy work tasks the same way. Hand them off to other people so you can do the work that only you are capable of.

Delegating helps you avoid the trap of multitasking. While you're going to have many different responsibilities at any given time, trying to constantly switch your focus between each task is exhausting and a poor use of your energy. Rather than getting multiple tasks done in less time, "studies show that people are most productive when they focus on doing just one thing" (Santomassimo, n.d., para. 2). When you pick up different tasks, your brain undergoes a brief adjustment period. Think about how hard it would be to answer history and math questions at the same time on an exam—as your brain struggles to shift gears, you lose your focus and sacrifice your productivity. Trying to take on two different tasks at once can set you back in the same way. You'll get better results, and you'll work more efficiently, if you finish one task before moving on to another.

One more way to make sure you're using your time wisely is to pay attention to how much time you're spending on customers. It might be worth the extra effort to make sure your company lands a high-paying customer who will generate a lot of business, but if you're spending multiple days negotiating with customers who contribute very little to your business, you're spending a lot of time on something that doesn't provide much benefit. If you can, pass some of these lower-paying customers off to other employees who have been trained to handle customer service. This frees you up to focus on the customers who will make or break your business.

Plan of Reorganization

The plan of reorganization is the act or process of restructuring a current, new or pre-existing plan, to bring it to the next level. It is sometimes necessary to make changes to plans, once you start working towards your goals. You may find that your current strategy isn't getting you the results you want. Rather than continuing forward with a plan you know isn't working, it's better to stop, take a look at your plan, and see where you can make adjustments.

The plan of reorganization isn't just for plans that aren't performing as intended; it can also be used for plans you have already followed and used to achieve your goals. Once you hit your targets, keep pushing. Revisit your plan and see how you can increase your goals to bring you even greater success. Whether you have a faulty plan, an underperforming plan, or a successful plan that you have surpassed, reorganizing will help you create a new strategy to achieve more than what you initially planned.

Reorganization is critically important whether you're the owner of a CDL business or the President of the United States. One of the most well-known and effective uses of reorganization was the Reorganization Act of 1939, which was a congressional act carried out by Franklin D. Roosevelt around the time of the New Deal. The act allowed the president to "hire six assistants, propose reorganization plans subject to congressional veto, and make economy in government a priority," (Cengage, 2020, para. 2) and it eventually led to the establishment of the Executive Office. It was a big reorganization of the executive branch of the government. It allowed Roosevelt to enact many important policies that helped him pursue the vision he had for the nation, and it has done the same for generations of presidents after him. This reorganization was so important and so powerful that it is still in place today, affecting how our government is structured nearly 80 years later.

Of course, presidents aren't the only ones capable of reorganizing their plans. In finances, a reorganization plan is performed for businesses that have filed a chapter 11 bankruptcy. These plans describe "the process of how an insolvent company will change structurally to help it pay its debts and stay in business" (Farlex Financial Dictionary, 2012, para. 1). In order to pay off debts, things need to change in the business. Blindly continuing with the old plan of operation is exactly what led to bankruptcy in the first place. In order to mend the damage, reorganization and developing a new strategy is key.

You can make use of the valuable practice of reorganization long before you're facing potential bankruptcy. If a plan isn't working, or if it isn't working well enough, there's nothing wrong with changing it up and finding a new plan that better suits your needs. Shifting focus as soon as a problem becomes apparent will save you lots of wasted time and energy.

Mastering the Three PORs for Power, Security, and Freedom

Mastering the PORs is all about finding balance between them. For the power of reset, it's good to take a step back and refocus yourself on your goals, but spending too long thinking about what you're going to do can get in the way of actually doing it. When it comes to the profit of return, you want to cut out the unnecessary work in your schedule, but you still need to remain involved with your company to ensure it continues to grow. As for the plan of reorganization, this is a useful tool for fixing or expanding upon plans, but don't get caught in the planning stage forever. Remember to also take action once you've optimized your plan to the best of your ability; you can always make adjustments later on.

If you can find a comfortable balance with all three PORs, you will be right in the sweet spot that affords you the greatest power, security, and freedom in your business.

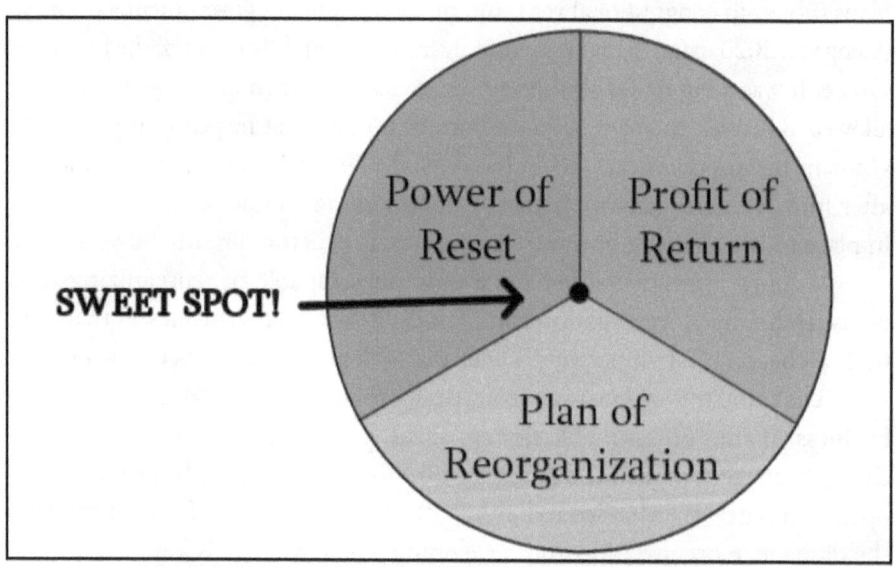

Additionally, pay attention to the way the three PORs tie into each other. Each POR creates a feedback loop with the others. The power of reset helps you clear your mind and focus your thoughts on your goals. Once you've done that, it is easier to make use of the plan of reorganization. Your goals are already in the forefront of your mind, so it's easier to see how you can restructure your plan to achieve them. When you've laid out your plan, use the profit of return strategy to make sure you're delegating each task in your plan appropriately. When you are only working on the tasks that provide the most benefit for your business, you are always focused on your big goals, which makes it even easier to use the power of reset. Each of the PORs leads into the next, creating a feedback loop that results in greater productivity and greater success.

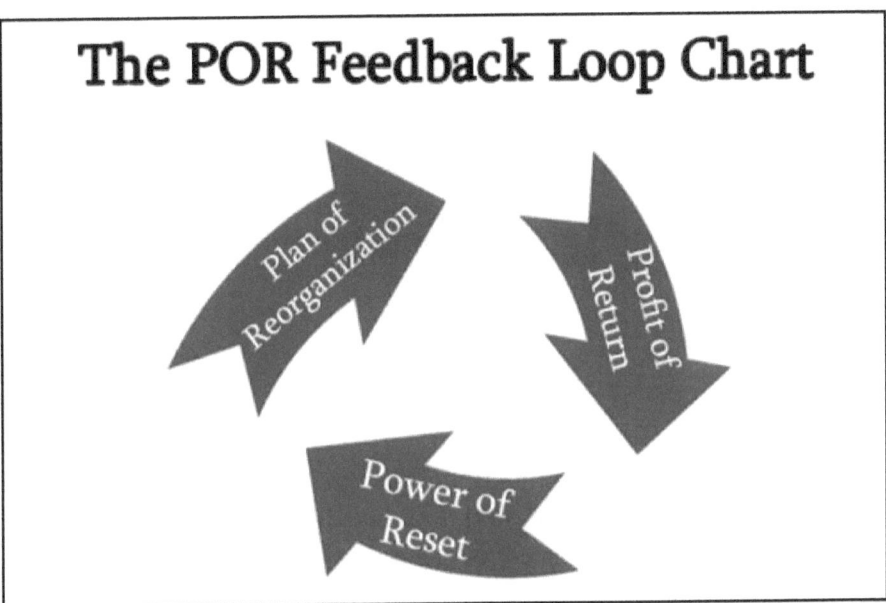

The POR Feedback Loop Chart

Plan of Reorganization

Profit of Return

Power of Reset

It is crucial to know, understand, and apply these PORs in your business. When you do, you support your goal-oriented mindset, and you constantly bring yourself closer to your goals. Along with the three POIs, these strategies can help you achieve unlimited freedom in everything you do.

CHAPTER
6

Maximizing Security Now for the Long Run

You might not think of CDL jobs as being especially dangerous, but many of them are actually full of potential security concerns. When you're driving around with hundreds or thousands of dollars' worth of goods in the back of your truck, it is no surprise that this poses a security risk. Other risks that can occur on the job are often related to long nights spent on the road, where exhausted drivers could pose a safety risk to themselves and others. There are also potential safety concerns for drivers that have to sleep in roadside motels or, worse, in their trucks when there aren't any motels with truck parking in sight.

As the owner of a CDL company, it is your responsibility to make sure both the driver and the goods arrive at their destination safely. Security concerns can lead to lost profits, lost customers, and even a shortage of employees. If drivers perceive their job as unsafe, they're less likely to stick with it. Take steps early to ensure your company is operating as safely as possible so you have these systems in place for the long run.

But what can you do to limit these security concerns and make sure your business is as safe as possible? Handling the issues begins with understanding the unique security threats posed to truck drivers and others in the CDL industry.

The Security Crisis in the CDL Trucking Industry

Trucking is the backbone of delivery services. Without truckers and others in the CDL industry, it would be impossible to ship things across the country for the low rates we currently enjoy. Despite this, there is a shortage of CDL-certified drivers that only worsens each year. Current estimates suggest that in the US alone, driver shortages are nearing 60,000 truckers, and "within the next eight years the shortage is predicted to reach a staggering 174,000" (Braw, 2018, para. 2). These driver shortages are partially a result of people perceiving the job as unsafe, which may discourage them from getting their CDL license.

Without new hires, security concerns only grow, creating a real security crisis. Here are a few of the biggest security issues in the CDL industry today.

Exhaustion

With fewer drivers in the industry than what is needed, the drivers who do work are often asked to work longer shifts later into the night. Driver exhaustion is a huge safety risk for any CDL company. The large size of most trucks means that a brief lapse of attention could lead to serious injury or even a deadly accident. Longer drives, especially those that are overnight, can seriously jeopardize your employees' safety.

Another side effect of the employee shortage are improperly trained employees. If drivers don't get the training they need to operate their vehicles safely, including going through any additional licensing procedures, they could be unfamiliar with their job duties and make more mistakes, especially if they are overworked. The consequences of these mistakes can range from relatively benign to very dangerous.

Expensive Cargo

If you're shipping expensive cargo, you're going to have concerns over its safety. This could mean shipping a few pricey things, or it could mean packing a truck full of less expensive items that add up to be worth much more. The more your cargo is worth, the greater the risk of it potentially getting stolen. An attempted theft could put your drivers at risk too depending on what they are shipping. Securing your cargo and reducing the risk of theft helps your employees feel safe.

Theft and Fraud

Just as theft can occur from outside the company, so too can it occur within the company. While you may want to think the best of your employees, the unfortunate truth is that some fraud is committed by people who work for the company they're stealing from. This kind of theft can be hard to police in the CDL industry, as drivers spend days at a time alone with just the cargo. One way to counteract it is to keep strict logs of what was shipped out and what arrived at its destination so you can spot any missing cargo right away. Keeping a close eye on your finances is another good way to reduce the chances of theft, and proper security training for all employees can limit the risk of fraud.

How to Overcome Liability and Work With Your Assets

Knowing the possible sources of security issues is only half the battle. The other half comes in the form of reducing the risk of security crises that negatively impact your business. Some solutions deal with recouping losses after an accident or theft has occurred, while others address the underlying issues that cause or allow for accidents and theft in the first place.

One method for reducing liability for accidents is buying insurance. This helps protect you from financial losses due to on-the-job accidents or destruction of company property. It can help you recover your losses, so they don't interfere with the health of your business. However, insurance only helps once a breach of security has occurred. While it's still a good idea, you should also look into ways to protect your cargo and your drivers before any theft or accidents have the chance to happen by lowering the chances of these safety hazards.

TWIC Cards

An increase in security concerns has led to the usage of Transportation Worker Identification Credential (TWIC) cards, which are typically required for drivers that come into contact with port facilities. TWIC cards "contain biometric information (human characteristics such as fingerprints) on a microchip, a magnetic strip, and a bar code, and require special reading devices for clearance and verification," (TruckingTruth, 2017, para. 5) and cardholders must also undergo a background check. While these security measures are extensive, they help to ensure the right people are getting access to secure facilities, and they limit the risk of fraud. Most over the road (OTR) drivers should get TWIC cards, so they can make and pick up shipments from secure maritime facilities. TWIC cards can also provide verified identification for these drivers at other locations.

Specific CDL Licenses and Endorsements

You must ensure that all of your drivers have the proper CDL licenses and endorsements for their jobs. Without them, they may lack the proper training and certification for the work they're doing. This can increase the risk of accidents and also increase your liability if an accident does occur.

The three different types of CDL licenses are categorized as Class A, Class B, and Class C. Each one allows license holders to perform different operations, and the training for each type of license is a little different.

Class A licenses are for combination vehicles like tractor-trailers. License holders can operate "any combination of vehicles that have a Gross Combination Weight Rating (GCWR) of 26,001 pounds or more," including towed units "with a gross vehicle weight of over 10,000 pounds" (Winnesota, 2018, para. 21). Class B licenses are for single vehicles of the same measurements, and Class C licenses allow for the operation of smaller vehicles with specialized purposes. These purposes include transporting 16 or more people or transporting hazardous waste.

On top of the different licenses, make sure your drivers have all necessary endorsements. These are necessary for certain jobs that are bigger safety hazards, and they typically require additional security screenings and a background check.

Applying Security in Your Business, Job, and Company

Safety and security should be a priority for your company. You should work to minimize the risk of workplace accidents wherever possible, and you should also limit the chances for theft or fraud to occur. Taking precautions early and following all safety guidelines will save you a lot of trouble in the long run.

If you maximize your security now, even if you only have a handful of employees, you won't have to worry about it as your business grows. You can maintain the same safety regulations and just scale them up to account for your business' growth. Take security measures seriously from day one to protect your assets so you don't end up a victim of theft. When you apply security in all aspects of your business, you protect yourself from future losses.

Overall Mindset Approach

Security concerns interfere with your long-term goals. Every security breach sets you back from where you want to be on your path to success. Every exhausted employee makes it harder to stick to the mission and vision statements you made when you founded your company. Security should be a key part of your mindset and your goals if you want to continue working towards your life's purpose.

Manage safety concerns as soon as they appear, and work to minimize security risks before they can become a problem. If you maintain a safe working atmosphere, it will be much easier to focus on achieving your overarching goals. Reduce your risk of liability for accidents, not just by protecting yourself legally and financially with insurance but also by reducing the risk of accidents. This makes your business a safer place to work, builds trust with your employees, and helps you reduce potential obstacles in order to achieve unlimited freedom as a CDL business owner and entrepreneur.

STEP 3

Living the CDL-Minded Lifestyle

The Value of Balancing Work, Family, and Play in Your Life

Our culture tends to praise workaholics. We correlate success with hard work, which means that if we want to be successful, we believe we have to spend every waking moment working for that success. However, is this really true, or is the celebration of the workaholic actually doing more harm than good?

To be sure, there must be hard work in every success. You're not going to launch your own CDL business without facing some challenges and putting in the effort to overcome them. Still, focusing on work to the exclusion of all other aspects of your life isn't healthy, and it's not as fulfilling as living a well-balanced life. In fact, rather than reducing your productivity, taking some time to relax can actually help you be more productive when you're working. We need to have downtime in our lives, and we need to walk the careful tightrope that is work-life balance.

Our lives should be full of work, family, and play, not just one or two of these aspects. Each contributes to a positive, healthy mindset, and learning to balance them all successfully keeps us productive and fulfilled.

The Importance of Work, Family, and Play

Work, family, and play are all necessary components of a happy and satisfying life. If you work until you feel ready to drop, you never get the chance to enjoy the fruits of your labor, and you can burn out quickly. If you focus only on living for your family, you might put personal and career goals aside, even if you still desire those goals. If you only ever play, you miss out on all the other experiences life has to offer through work and family. Each aspect is important to our lives, and each one plays a key role in keeping us well-rounded.

Some people see work as just something that pays the bills, and in many industries and jobs, that tends to be the case when it comes to work. However, when you run your own CDL company, work becomes much more than that. It is a way to achieve financial freedom, but it is also a way for us to feel a sense of purpose in our lives. It gives us a way to direct our efforts and make progress towards our life's purpose. Remember that work isn't limited to just our jobs. It can also encompass personal projects we take on and any volunteer work we do for others. When we feel like we are making a positive difference with our work, we experience the greatest levels of professional and personal satisfaction.

Spending time with our families is equally important to our well-being. Too much work can interfere with your personal life, which can keep you from seeing your family as often as you would like. You might miss important milestones and parties, which can strain your personal relationships. When we share time with our families, we grow closer as a family unit, and we reinforce our motivation for working. We start to see success not just as something that benefits us but also as something that benefits our families.

Play is often perceived as less important than work or family time, but it is actually crucial to our mental and emotional health. Hobbies and other fun activities engage us outside of work. They give us a way to de-stress at the end of the day and take our minds off of our work. Spending leisure time with friends also helps us feel more connected to them and fulfills our need for socialization. Group activities like playing a board game or video game together, going on a walk or hike, and practicing hobbies together are all great ways to share our recreational time with others.

When we take some time away from work to play or spend time with our families, we get to enjoy what all of our efforts have brought us. Work seems more purposeful because we know what it's helping us to achieve. Play and family time reinforces our goals, and we put these goals into motion at work. We are more motivated and it is easier to continue striving towards success.

Working Smarter, Not Harder

Spending too much time at work can reduce the amount of time you have available for family and leisure time. When you have a lot of things you need to get done and not much time to do them in, how do you manage all of your responsibilities? The solution is learning to work smarter, not harder. We've already discussed time management and how to leverage your time effectively, but there are many more solutions you can use to reduce your workload just by changing the way you work. You can get the same amount of work done in a fraction of the time and energy you would otherwise spend on it with these habits and tricks. This frees up your schedule and fixes your work-life balance without allowing any important tasks to fall by the wayside.

Invite Feedback

Feedback often uncovers the bad and negative habits that cause us to work hard instead of working smart. Other people are usually much better at pointing out our flaws than we are, and they can identify areas where we're wasting time and working inefficiently. Look for feedback on any task you have difficulty with, especially if you can ask a mentor or expert in the area. Even if you think you're great at something, you can almost always improve, and these improvements will save you a lot of time and effort.

The best feedback is specific and actionable. Remember that just because someone is an expert in their field, this doesn't mean they're an expert at giving advice. Some of the burden falls on you to ask the right questions. Point out specific parts of the task that are difficult for you and ask questions not just about what's wrong but how you can improve. When you improve the quality of your work (and learn a few tips from experts while you're at it), you won't have to spend nearly as long workshopping and revisiting tasks. If you have the time to fix something, it takes even less time to get it right on the first try.

Practice Being Concise

A lot more time is wasted in being long-winded than you might think. If you sit and stew over the best way to write a one-line email, you've turned a 10-minute task into a half-hour-long one. If you're speaking to a customer and you waste time explaining a ton of information that doesn't matter for the sale, you can double the time you spend meeting with people, not to mention making it harder for them to pay attention to the part of your speech that's actually relevant to them.

Being concise helps you get your point across clearer, which minimizes confusion. When you are brief and blunt where appropriate, it's easier for others to understand what you're saying and follow your directions. You don't need to be so brief you come off as rude, but you don't need to go running to the thesaurus every time you write a memo either. While million-dollar words might make you sound smarter on the surface, they can get in the way of getting your message across. Why say "fallacious" when you could simply say "wrong"? People will know what you are saying, which makes you a more efficient communicator.

Keep Learning

There is always so much more to learn, both as a business owner and as a person. The more you learn, the more you can apply your new knowledge to your work. Becoming an expert in your field helps you keep your business competitive, and it helps you narrow down your focus to the work that matters.

When you stop learning, you limit your potential for growth. You spend just as long on tasks after years of practice as you did when you first started doing them. You waste time making improvements in areas of your business that won't help you attract more customers. Learning is what keeps your head above water as a business owner. Continue developing your skills and trying to improve your efficiency every day. Learn to do things the easy way and you'll save yourself a lot of hassle.

Avoid Overworking Yourself

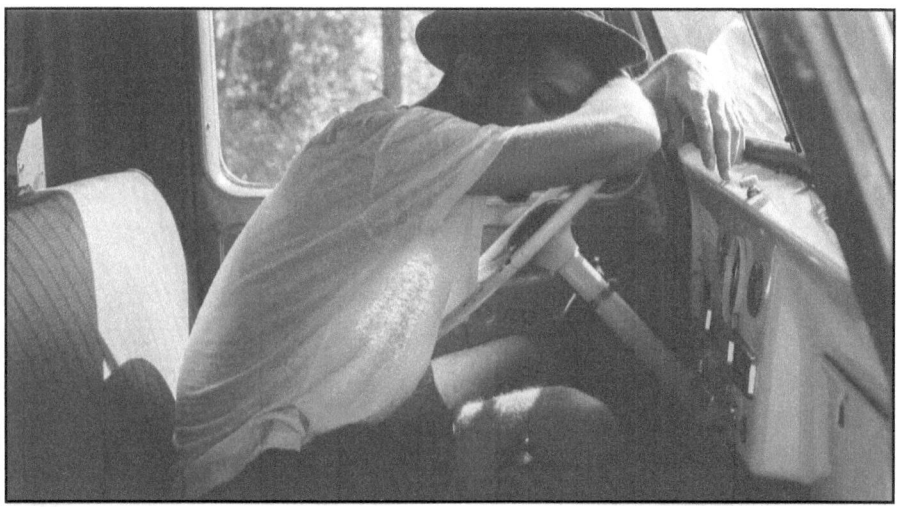

You can't work hard all the time. If you do, you will only burn out quickly. Your work quality will suffer, you'll feel unmotivated to finish even small tasks, and you'll have a hard time really caring about what you're doing. If you convince yourself that the only way to achieve your goals is to work hard all the time without any breaks, achieving your goals won't sound so desirable after all.

Take breaks when you need them throughout the workday. If you finish a difficult task, give yourself five or 10 minutes to rest before jumping into the next thing. Avoid bringing work home with you, physically or mentally. If you get home and you find you're still thinking about work, you're effectively still in "work mode" which makes it impossible to actually relax. You need to find time for leisure and time for family in your schedule or you put your motivation at risk.

Find Time to Relax With Your Family

It can be hard to organize shared family time. Kids have school, clubs, sports, hobbies, and time spent with their friends. Your spouse likely has a job and hobbies of their own. Other relatives like parents and siblings may have busy schedules too. Despite these difficulties, it is still crucial to spend time with your family and make lasting memories with each other.

Family time is more than just sitting and watching TV together. Strive for shared experiences that bring your family together and reinforce the values you want to teach your kids. This could mean playing a game, doing an activity together like cooking or camping, having open and honest conversations, or even just finding the time to have dinner together.

Why Family Time Matters

One of the most important benefits of family time is also one of the most straightforward. When you are more present in your family, you reinforce the family bonds. If you're never around, it's easy to feel like the family is destabilized. Long nights at work mean you're missing from a lot of important life events. Just making an effort to leave work on time shows your family you care about them and brings you closer together.

Shared family experiences can also help teach kids important lessons. Kids learn a lot of their early behaviors from their surroundings, and their parents in particular. If you want to teach them good behaviors, spending time with them is the best way to do so. More family time can help kids foster a positive mindset, improve their academic grades, and much more. They will build important skills that they will put into practice their whole lives.

Finally, family time reminds you what you are working for. Money isn't just a tool to have an easier life. It's also a way to give the people you love a better life. It's a way for you to provide for them and make sure their lives are as happy and fulfilling as your own. This can motivate you to work even harder as you remind yourself why your work matters.

Make Time for Recreation

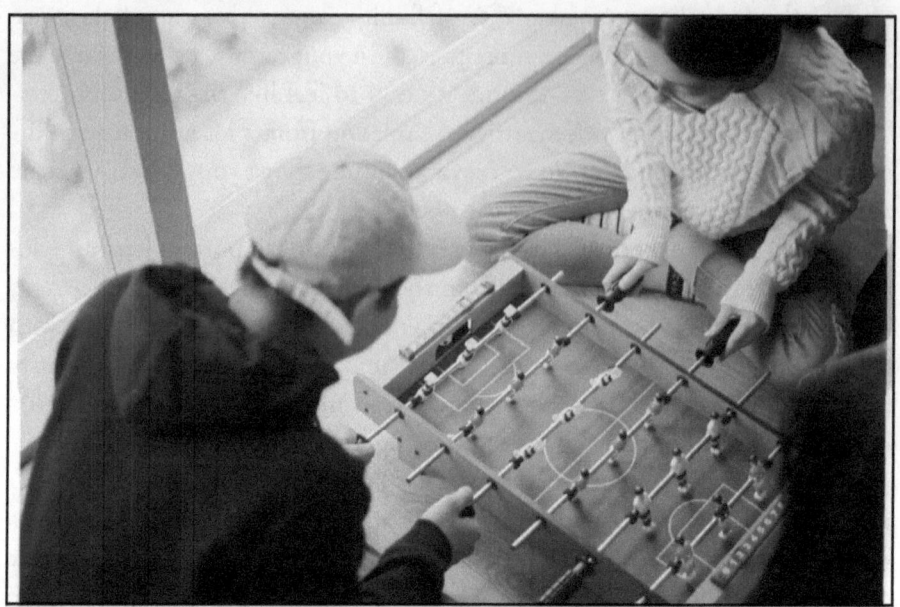

Play doesn't have to end just because you're an adult. In fact, it's actually good for adults to continue to seek out opportunities for recreation in their lives. Recreation functions as stress relief and helps take your mind off of difficulties you may be facing at work or in other areas of your life. It gives you a way to cope with difficult emotions and puts you in a more positive state of mind. When you take some time for leisure, you can return to work refreshed and ready to go. Playing also helps you get the creative juices flowing, which can improve your decision-making at work.

One of the easiest ways to fit more fun into your life is to add it to your schedule like you do work. This might not be the most spontaneous way to play, but it ensures that you'll take playtime as seriously as you do working hours. Doing something fun each day is just as important for your productivity as setting aside time to focus on work, so you should treat it with the same weight on your schedule.

If you're running low on time, try making other activities (that you need to get done) more fun. For example, if you exercise every day, choose an exercise you enjoy and that feels more like play than work, or get your daily fitness goals in by playing a sport. Make work a little more fun by introducing events like pizza parties and team-building activities. See where you can make your time at work a little more lively and make a conscious effort to have a little more fun every day.

Overall Lifestyle Approach

A good balance of work and leisure will make you much more productive in the long run. You will have an easier time achieving your goals, and when you are well-rested, you will come into work with a clearer head, ready to tackle whatever the day throws at you. Take every opportunity to remind yourself why your work matters and what it helps you achieve, whether this means carving out family time or enjoying your newfound free time.

Instead of living a life that is all work and no play, turn work into play. You can cut down on harmful habits like procrastination by making tasks more fun. Pure and simple fun is an amazing motivator. Take the example of the piano stairs that were installed in a subway station which were engineered so "as people climbed up the stairs, each step would play a different musical note" (Fabrega, 2013, para. 8). Even this tiny change encouraged more people to take the stairs, a task which they might otherwise have avoided. Make unpleasant tasks just a little more fun and you'll finish them faster and with a better mindset, embracing both work and play into your life.

CHAPTER

8

Embrace Constant Change

"The only thing constant is change"
—Heraclitus of Ephesus

Change is inevitable. No matter how much experience you have or how evergreen your niche, you will experience change in some form or another. Some businesses try to stick with what they know, failing to accommodate the change and losing business as a result. Others will try to keep up with new development but won't know how to stay relevant in an ever-changing marketplace. Understanding trends in your market and adapting to change as it happens is the only way to ensure that your business continues to thrive for years to come.

If you don't change with the times, the world will leave you behind. Embracing change is mandatory for any business. Constant evolution and adaptation will help your business keep up with new developments and remain competitive. Rather than fighting against change, welcome it, as it represents a new opportunity to grow and expand your company.

Changes and Challenges in the CDL Industry

Being able to predict changes in your market keeps you ahead of the curve. When you know change is coming, it is much easier to adjust your business strategy and your goals to match. We're not able to stop or reverse time, as much as we might want to. We can only affect how we react or respond to life's many inevitable changes.

While you can't predict the future, you can focus on certain aspects of the CDL industry that are constantly experiencing changes. Keep a close eye on new trends in these areas and consider how they might affect your business. Try to stay proactive in your responses to these trends so you aren't left behind when they occur.

Shifting Markets

A shifting market can make or break your company. Businesses that operate seasonally or only in certain weather conditions are at a greater risk of change than most, as business will fluctuate wildly throughout the year. If you're unprepared for these changes, they can leave you scrambling to break even on operating costs in the off-season.

Still, even the most reliable markets don't last forever. While commercial driving itself is a relatively stable industry—transporting goods through trucking has been around since the late 1800s and isn't likely to disappear—the more specific niches in each market may come and go. As a small business, you might focus on a single region or a certain transportation niche that could very well change in the next few years. It's best to watch for early warning signs of changes in your niche and react as early as possible.

Changes in Vehicles and Other Equipment

As years go by, vehicles break down and become outdated. The type of trucks, buses, vans, or shuttles you use now will probably not still be in use a decade into the future. The same is true for a lot of the other equipment your CDL business may use.

Upgrading to newer vehicles and equipment can be a costly expense, but it's a necessary one. Old vehicles can become unsafe over time and standards for equipment safety may change. Luckily, this change rarely occurs without plenty of warning. If you anticipate your vehicles becoming outdated and you save enough money ahead of time to replace your fleet, you shouldn't have too many difficulties adapting to this kind of change.

New Tax Laws and Regulations

Governments are constantly updating tax codes, many of which will affect you as a small business owner. Some of these changes will benefit you, giving you more opportunities for tax breaks. Others will saddle you with higher taxes which could become a big problem if you can't find ways to keep your business profitable. Thoroughly reviewing new tax laws will help you understand how the changes apply to you and how you can take advantage of any new tax breaks.

Legal regulations for CDL businesses may change over time as well. Pay attention to federal, state, and city laws regarding how and where your business can operate, and follow any new changes as quickly as possible. The fine you might receive for violating a regulation is much worse than the minor inconvenience of changing your operation strategy.

How to Manage Change

If change is going to happen whether you want it to or not, how do you learn to manage it? It's hard to transition your business to a new plan for operation, but if you don't, you put your company's success in jeopardy. Long-term success requires you to recognize, address, and respond to change effectively. The best ways to accomplish this is to start expecting change and to try to see change in a more positive light.

Learn to Expect Change

Change catches us off-guard if we don't learn to expect it. This can make it much harder to adjust to our new circumstances, especially if we grow too attached to our old ones. While we'll likely always feel some nostalgia for the early days of our businesses, we need to accept that our lives can turn on a dime. Something we take for granted today could be taken away from us tomorrow. This hurts most when we cling desperately to the past, but it's not so painful when we start to see it coming.

When you start expecting change to occur, you mentally prepare yourself for it. Keeping track of new trends isn't just a way to maximize your income. You adjust your mindset, which helps you see change as a promising opportunity rather than a burden.

See Change as an Opportunity

Change doesn't have to be a negative force in your life. Instead, it can represent a great new opportunity to expand your business into new markets, increase your profits, and try something new. It might disrupt your life a bit, but if nothing ever changed, life would be pretty boring.

Change gives you a chance to test the waters of new markets and try out different goals. It can be the encouragement you need to go out on a limb and attempt something you wouldn't have otherwise. You've already used change for this exact purpose. After all, becoming a CDL entrepreneur is a big change in your life, but it's a change that is well worth it. Your life wouldn't be the same if you had decided to reject change and allow the opportunity to run your own business pass you by. Embracing change can help you accomplish things that you never thought were possible.

Overall CDL-Minded Approach

Fear of the unknown is natural. It's completely normal to worry about potential changes in the market that could affect the way you run your business. Uncertainty and doubt are common when starting something new. However, these feelings don't have to hold you back if you don't let them. A little bit of fear is necessary for real, lasting change. It means you're trying something you've never done before that has the opportunity to turn your life around.

If you learn to anticipate and accept change, you will have a much easier time adjusting to it. Identify what changes you will need to make ahead of time. This will let you put yourself in a good position for adjusting to the change as smoothly and effectively as possible. With the right mindset and sufficient preparation, there is no change you can't overcome.

Appendix

Common Marketing Terminology

- Brand awareness: the extent to which people can recognize and remember your company
- Call to action: a request for a reader or listener to complete a certain action
- Digital marketing: marketing that occurs online
- Key performance indicator (KPI): any variable measured to show how well your business is performing in a certain area
- Market trends: changes in a specific industry or field over time
- Remarketing: reconnecting with people who have shown interest in or used your service before
- Return on investment (ROI): a measure for evaluating the effectiveness of a marketing strategy or other investment relative to its cost
- Word-of-mouth marketing: marketing that occurs through recommendation of your services from a satisfied customer to other potential customers

CDL Trade Publications

- Advanced Transportation Technology News
- American Shipper Magazine
- American Trucker
- Bulk Transporter
- Business Examiner
- Commercial Motor
- Fleet Executive
- Keep on Truckin' News

- Logistics & Transport Focus
- Modern Bulk Transporter
- Road King Magazine
- The Trucker
- World of Truckers

Trade Associations and Industry Events for Networking

- Accelerate! Conference and Expo
- American Trucking Association Management Conference & Exhibition
- CVSA Annual Conference and Exhibition
- CVTA Conference
- Mid-America Trucking Show
- National Association of Fleet Administration Annual Institute & Expo
- National Association of Small Trucking Companies
- Omnitracs Outlook
- The Work Truck Show
- TMC Annual

Templates

Trucking Business Plan Templates

- General Freight Trucking Business Plan (https://www.bplans.com/general_freight_trucking_business_plan/executive_summary_fc.php)
- General Motor Freight Trucking Business Plan (https://www.bplans.com/general_motor_freight_trucking_business_plan/executive_summary_fc.php)
- Limousine Taxi Business Plan (https://www.bplans.com/limousine_taxi_business_plan/executive_summary_fc.php)

- Taxi Business Plan ((https://www.bplans.com/taxi_business_plan/executive_summary_fc.php)
- Truck Stop Business Plan (https://www.bplans.com/truck_stop_business_plan/executive_summary_fc.php)

Budget Calculation Templates

- Quickbooks: budget template (https://quickbooks.intuit.com/r/budgeting/essential-small-business-financial-tools-free-startup-budget-template-and-guide/)
- Smartsheet: marketing budget templates (https://www.smartsheet.com/12-free-marketing-budget-templates)

References

Beck, J. (n.d.). *Family standing on the beach.* Unsplash. https://unsplash.com/photos/a-nWU0o73r4

Blake, J. (2017, Mar. 13). *What is your happiness formula?* OWN. http://www.oprah.com/inspiration/jenny-blake-what-is-your-happiness-formula#ixzz5cypGE6w9

Braw, E. (2018, Sept. 19). *Trucking is the security crisis you never noticed.* Foreign Policy. https://foreignpolicy.com/2018/09/19/trucking-is-the-security-crisis-you-never-noticed/

Briscoe, J. (n.d.). *Checking stocks.* Unsplash. https://unsplash.com/photos/Gw_sFen8VhU

Carstens-Peters, G. (n.d.). *Writing a checklist.* Unsplash. https://unsplash.com/photos/RLw-UC03Gwc

Cengage. (2020, May 27). *Reorganization Act of 1939.* Encyclopedia.com. https://www.encyclopedia.com/economics/encyclopedias-almanacs-transcripts-and-maps/reorganization-act-1939

Crawford, R. (n.d.). *Wood truck on the road.* Unsplash. https://unsplash.com/photos/99HLgU4IHLY

Cussen, M. P. (2020, Jan. 30). *How will your investment make money?* Investopedia. https://www.investopedia.com/articles/financial-theory/09/how-investments-make-money-income.asp

DeLawrence, O. (n.d.). *Tax statements.* Unsplash. https://unsplash.com/photos/5616whx5NdQ

Entrepreneur. (2016, June 6). *The legal ABCs of running a transportation service.* https://www.entrepreneur.com/article/273812

Farlex Financial Dictionary. (2012). *Plan of reorganization.* https://financial-dictionary.thefreedictionary.com/Plan+of+Reorganization

Farrow, J. (n.d.). *Truck driving at dawn.* Unsplash. https://unsplash.com/photos/ucuOscdCaO4

Free-Photos. (2015, Sept. 7). *Sharpened pencil.* Pixabay. https://pixabay.com/photos/pencil-sharpener-notebook-paper-918449/

G-Town. (n.d.). *The freedom of trucking: Blessing or curse?* TruckingTruth. https://www.truckingtruth.com/trucking_blogs/Article-3898/the-freedom-of-trucking

Incorporate.com. (n.d.). *Start a trucking company in eight steps.* https://www.incorporate.com/learning-center/start-trucking-company-eight-steps/

Janssens, E. (n.d.). *Coffee and a monthly planner.* Unsplash. https://unsplash.com/photos/aQfhbxailCs

Kirb, L. (n.d.). *Asleep at the wheel.* Unsplash. https://unsplash.com/photos/5tniytQs68E

Langford, S. (n.d.). *Timex analog clock.* Unsplash. https://unsplash.com/photos/eIkbSc3SDtI

Meyes, D. (n.d.). *Rusted tow truck.* Unsplash. https://unsplash.com/photos/XZQacH1x1rE

Moran, J. (n.d.). *Man standing on a cliff.* Unsplash. https://unsplash.com/photos/hrEJYRtBDrk

Nizal, A. (n.d.). *Man running on the seashore.* Unsplash. https://unsplash.com/photos/L5Lt0e7Kjxc

Proctor, B. (2011, Nov. 6). *11 forgotten laws—The law of sacrifice* [Video]. YouTube. https://www.youtube.com/watch?v=NFienuvDsnY

Progressive Insurance. (n.d.). *Person looking at charts and graphs.* Unsplash. https://unsplash.com/photos/unRkg2jH1j0

Reyes, A. (n.d.). *Work flow chart.* Unsplash. https://unsplash.com/photos/qWwpHwip31M

Santomassimo, R. (n.d.). *3 steps to better utilizing your time for higher commissions.* The Massimo Group. https://massimo-group.com/time-utilization/

Shinn, F. S. (2005). *The Game of life and how to play it.* Florence Shinn.

Sincerely Media. (n.d.). *Glasses resting on a book.* Unsplash. https://unsplash.com/photos/c1YrcFYW66s

Souza, L. (n.d.). *Tour buses.* Unsplash. https://unsplash.com/photos/bAFWnhGAvxk

Tadyanehondo, N. (n.d.). *Aerial photo of freight trucks.* Unsplash. https://unsplash.com/photos/GOD2mDNujuU

Tantara. (2019, July 10). *Eleven reasons you should become a truck driver.* https://www.tantara.us/news/eleven-reasons-become-truck-driver/

TruckingTruth. (2017, Mar. 21). *TWIC cards.* https://www.truckingtruth.com/wiki/topic-45/twic-cards

Truong, B. (n.d.). *Man and woman playing foosball.* Unsplash. https://unsplash.com/photos/hYrnz92-bpY

Washington, D. (2017, Mar. 29). *Amazing motivational speech by Denzel Washington - Claim your dream 2017* [Video]. YouTube. https://www.youtube.com/watch?v=EBGb40yh4SY

Wicks, B. (n.d.). *Close-up photo of a watch.* Unsplash. https://unsplash.com/photos/kvzV9gHv1ic

Winnesota. (2018, Sept. 5). *CDL endorsements for commercial drivers: The ultimate guide.* https://www.winnesota.com/news/cdlendorsements

Ziglar, Z. (n.d.). *The Seven Steps of Goal Setting.* https://curvefinder.com/wp-content/uploads/2016/08/Goal-Setting-Canvas-1.pdf

CDL MINDED MARKETING

3-STEP SYSTEM TO **BUILD**,
ESTABLISH, AND **GROW** YOUR BRAND
IN **YOUR BUSINESS** FOR **ENTREPRENEURS**,
SMALL BUSINESS OWNERS,
AND COMMERCIAL **DRIVER/OPERATORS**

JOE RYDER

INTRODUCTION

"I'm convinced that about half of what separates
successful entrepreneurs from the non-successful
ones is pure perseverance."
—*Steve Jobs*

When did you first believe you wanted to be an entrepreneur?

Have you known it your whole life, or did a certain experience lure you into the world of trucking?

All of us know, the trucking lifestyle isn't easy, so it certainly wasn't because you wanted to put in your 14 hours on the road and then kick back for a 6-hour nap, only to get up and do it all again.

Something inside your heart and perhaps a force inside your soul called you to pursue this occupation and this way of life. Some even refer to it as a 'calling' they feel when they get in the cab and face the open road. But it doesn't stop there.

You know how to maneuver a quarter ton 'box of bricks' in the tightest of dock areas; you can sleep at any time of the day; and you can navigate a big city with your eyes closed.

There's a certain way of thinking and 'feeling' which is in every driver's blood; it's there when you schedule a long haul and it's there when you finally get a shower after a 4-day run. It's there when you're driving in the morning with the whole world out in front of you just waiting to be experienced, and it's there when you are on the dark, quiet highway, in the middle of nowhere, wondering what your family and friends are doing.

And now, you've decided to drive for yourself. The industry is second nature to you now and you feel you're ready to offer customers something new, something improved, or maybe it's just that you want to improve *your* life—be your own boss, manage a skilled team, with new ideas and a new set of rules for operating a business.

When it comes to setting up a successful company, there are basics which need to be in place, decisions that have to be made.

Do you want to cover just a specific region?

Are you going to cater to a targeted industry, such as livestock or refrigeration?

Do you have nimble trucks which will only deliver within city blocks, or are you an expert at managing double and triple trailers for interstate loads?

Or are you wanting the entire pie, covering every specialty imaginable so you can get as many trips scheduled as possible?

When considering all the possibilities and commitments, it's easy to feel overwhelmed. Not only do you want to satisfy your customers, but you should be in it to improve your life too, whether by making more money, being able to govern your own schedule, or moving into management and having your own crew of drivers.

Within these pages are the nuggets you'll need to begin your profitable CDL/trucking business. The methods will help you to discover your focus and will lead you to choosing your branding strategy, which, if done correctly, will lead into a marketing strategy that you will custom fit for your business. After you have picked the marketing channels that not only find most comfortable with, but that will give you the results you are looking for, your marketing strategy will be set and finding your ideal customers will just be a matter of putting the strategy in motion.

You'll write your business' mission/vision statement, declaring the foundational values you'll build your company on. You will also find that having your mission statement close at hand can be a reminder of what you wanted your company to stand for and why you started it in the first place. There will be times which may challenge you and you'll be ready to junk the whole idea; having this statement close at hand can pull you back to basics and give you the reasons you need to rethink your future and move forward.

After you have written your mission and vision statements, it's time to assemble a business plan. This process has many components, and we'll guide you through the process as you learn the important role your business plan plays when organizing your company, and, when it's time, designing your marketing brand. It has a key role in the building of your company.

When you've laid the groundwork for your business and you're ready to move forward with devising a marketing plan, we'll discuss all the tools you can use, which will make finding your ideal customer easy. The process of getting your company in front of these businesses is paramount in catching their attention and eventually turning them into life-long customers will be explained with sample situations and understandable terms. It isn't as mysterious or unattainable as it might seem right now.

All strategies and channels you can use are taught in an easy-to-understand language, so you don't have to worry about being experienced in the field or having done it before. It also isn't grade-school dummied-down. When you finish, you'll wonder why you've been so apprehensive for so long. It can be easy!

The world of traditional and online advertising will open doors you had no idea existed, blending a couple of channels for a simple strategy to get your first customers, right up to a multi-launch campaign. The process is easy, and as you build your company image and develop ways to reach your customers, you will quickly gain the ability and know-how to mix TV ads with PPC promotions or blog postings with Facebook ads. The best part? You'll know exactly why you're combining each channel and for what intended outcome.

Finally, the ominous task of designing and launching a website will be simplified and explained, firstly with the benefits of how an informational site can almost run your business for you, and secondly, how easy it is to assemble and launch with a few knowledgeable tricks and your own computer or laptop.

When you finish this book, all the tools you'll need to begin your business strategy, from choosing how to develop a company logo to building loyal customer relationships, will be in your marketing strategy toolbox, and it will all be as simple to set into motion as counting to 3.

GLOSSARY OF MARKETING TERMS

Advertising - any means by which a business draws attention to potential customers for sales.

Affiliate marketing - a process where two people or businesses have an agreement to promote a product or service to their existing customers. If a recipient purchases a product or service, the promoter receives a percentage of the sale.

Blogging - typically, an online (usually recurring) journal entry or article of interest regarding a person's experience or opinion.

Campaign - a marketing blitz using multiple media tools to achieve an intended outcome.

Channel - a marketing method which uses optimal marketing options to achieve a preferred end result.

Customer awareness - recognition of a business, practice, or initiative within a community or industry by its customers.

Market presence - recognition of a business within its industry.

Multimedia - a combination of media that utilizes traditional and non-traditional methods, such as printed flyers, radio spots, Facebook ads, and website blogs.

Niche - a specific segment within an industry, having unique characteristics and nuances; can be defined as a purchaser demographic who would benefit the most from an offer.

PPC (pay per click) - an advertising tool used in online marketing, by which an established website sells ad space to a buyer and the buyer only pays if a viewer 'clicks' on their ad, which takes them to a promotional or landing page.

Promotions - a specific advertising strategy with a purpose to achieve sales.

Public relations - a method of promoting a company to community and civic groups and creating a network of common interest groups.

Strategy - an organized, long-term plan assembled with a specific goal in mind.

Social media - the industry as a whole, consisting of social sites such as Facebook, Twitter, etc., where members can interact and post media to theirs and other member pages.

Social networking - creating communication between people connecting on the Internet, usually with a common idea or goal.

Website - a location on the Internet where a person or business can present ideas, products, or services for others to view and interact with.

CHAPTER ONE

Strategy Will Win Over the Most Challenging of Circumstances

A s with any plan, putting your brand and marketing strategy together can seem overwhelming.

Don't let this intimidate you. The glossary in the front of this book is for your reference of the most common and often-used terms in business, marketing, advertising, and branding.

Starting your own business is a challenge, but you know your industry, you know what is needed behind the scenes to be successful. You also know that you can do this if you have the answers to, not only some, but to *all* of your questions. By discussing where our industry is now and some of our advantages and set-backs, a clearer image may give way to how quickly things change and how adapting to recent events can launch you in a direction you may not be aware of.

As 2020 began, the trucking industry was growing and had a lot of competition. Now more than ever, people have taken up the idea to start their own companies.

New customers are in need of transportation services who used other forms before the COVID-19 pandemic broke out. Many foundational industries, particularly retail and manufacturing, have used truck transportation exclusively and have found air transport to be affordable. Due to the fact that airlines are trying to make up lost revenue from clientele, many corporations have closed their businesses, rates have dropped and therefore truckers have lost their businesses and their clients. Still, other trucking lines have lost their revenue completely, even in the trade show markets, the esteemed and long-term clients have turned into ghosts, and are now trying to figure out new avenues and industries for themselves.

Everyone is maneuvering to make money where it's been lost, and as transportation professionals are in a bind trying to come up with solutions, we are the last line of defense to see who is in need and who is not.

But one thing is very clear:

The nation and the world needs CDL Minded professionals in the CDL industry.

Products and services will still have to move from one place to another.

And now, you believe you can offer these new (and previous) customers, new choices. So, let's get down to business and begin to build your company!

Assess Your Skills

- What do you do best?

- What can you offer that the 'other company' does not?

- Are your prices better?

- Do you guarantee your arrival dates?

- Are you a master at moving produce, steel machinery, or some other specialty you feel needs more attention?

Know Your Strengths and Your Weaknesses

- Do you like to crunch numbers and feel you're a natural in financial matters?

- Does building a website or social presence intimidate you?

- What things do you do that people compliment you on, or tell others to get in touch with you for?

- Does the thought of recording a video scare the living daylights out of you, or do you think it would be fun to develop a personality in your market and gather a following of like-minded customers?

Weigh the Specifics of Your Business and What You Want to Accomplish

- Do you have a goal in mind, like running goods for food shelters or delivering donations for Habitat for Humanity?

- Are you focused on having more money in the bank to help your family?

- Will having a stable client base give you the stability you're looking for in a world turned upside down?

After you've developed the basis of your business and know the ins and outs of moving forward, it's time to assemble the basics for building and running a successful company. By thinking of yourself as a 'business,' you have started the process of having a 'business mindset' which needs to be in place before building your image, or 'brand,' for marketing.

Getting in now with a new business or taking steps to further improve your existing company couldn't have come at a better time, believe it or not. A well-thought-out business strategy can sustainably work now, and also in the future.

Once you have listed your best skills, decide specifically on what you want to offer and have a good idea of who you want to offer it to; the rest will just be decisions and action. Ask yourself the following three questions:

1. How much money do you want to invest?

2. How many people will you have to reach in order for your business to be profitable?

3. How can you set up a campaign which will govern itself and only need occasional maintenance if you're on the road or want to take time off?

These considerations are part of the overall structure of your business framework. Your next steps in constructing a solvent business should include:

Writing a Business Plan - The old proverb still makes sense; if you don't know where you are going, how will you know when you get there? The same logic rings true for starting a business. Organize your thoughts. In *Step 1 of Building Your Brand*, you'll go through this process. There are specifics you'll want to make sure are set in stone, but others you may not be sure of, or even if they will be part of your plan. Don't worry—we'll get you there.

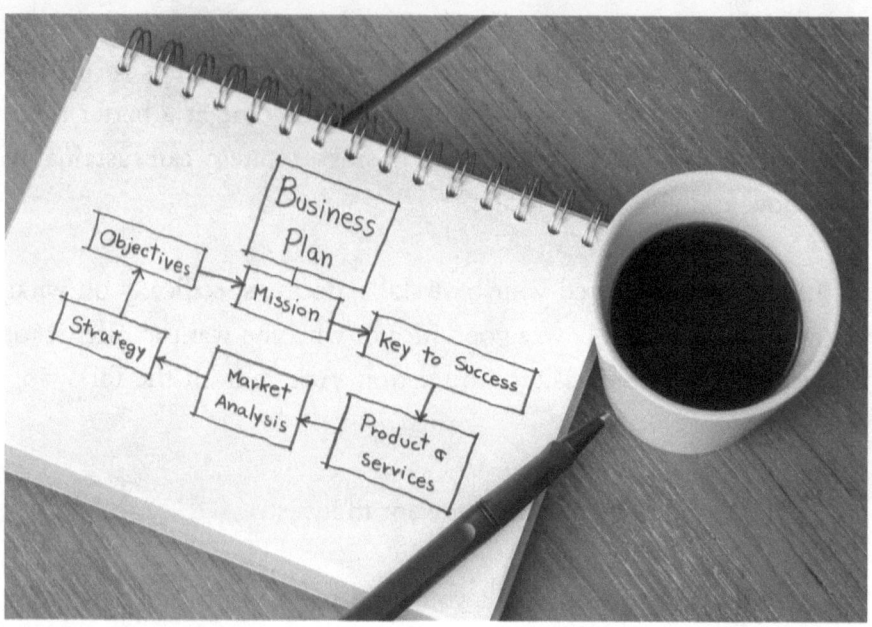

Establish Your Business, Legally - By implementing a Limited Liability Company, sole proprietorship, or corporation, you will be setting boundaries for your company and protecting yourself from liability or disastrous events. You will learn how each one works, the benefits and downfalls, and choose which structure will work best for you. Discussions later will include establishing a registered agent (not having one can jeopardize your business' operations by missing state mandate notices, tax documents, legal notices, or wage garnishments if you become distracted or forget to file). You'll learn why you should apply for an electronic identification number (EIN) for your business, which is required for you to open a banking account and will also be used on all tax identification for the life of your business. You'll learn about shareholders, partners, personal and business assets, and more. Protect your business, protect yourself.

Purchase and Possess All Business Licenses and Permits - Check with the state your office will reside in, and also any states you will be traveling to within your territory. In addition to the specific business license(s) you may need, you must also retain:

Commercial Driver's License (CDL) and any endorsements which may be needed - it is a Federal Law to have this.

Motor Carrier Operating Authority number - you may need more than one of these numbers for your business, depending on your specific operations.

USDOT Number - to identify all motor carriers when they conduct inspections, investigations or audits, the Federal Motor Carrier Safety Administration (FMCSA) uses a USDOT number, an assigned and unique number for each company.

International Registration Plan (IRP) credentials and an International Fuel Tax Agreement (IFTA) decal - if you operate in multiple states, you will need to obtain both of these credentials to be compliant.

Choose to Buy or Lease Your Equipment - Make sure your equipment can handle the freight you intend on delivering. When you are starting out, consider whether buying or leasing will suit your operation best.

Document Your Income and Expenses - There are numerous software programs which can make this task easy and also offer the needed reports to submit with payroll and tax claims. Choose one which will organize your entries best for a clear and understandable summary. Pick one you understand and can use easily, because you will be using it every day. Due to the many times your entry amounts and receipts are received at untimely rates, sometimes weeks and months after a delivery has been completed, it is important that this tool is as uncomplicated and user-friendly as possible.

Often, an accountant familiar with a trucking company's operation can start you off with the right tools and suggest the best way for you to handle your accounts. Having this advice can save you headaches down the road if you've used a complicated or non-compliant software, or have to re-count 6 months worth of entries.

Establish the way you'll be paid by your customers before you begin scheduling too, so both you and your clients are on the same page when you begin. Maintain complete records of all expenses before, during, and after the delivery. Keep personal and business expenses separated.

Purchase Appropriate Insurance - Compare pricing and make sure you have all areas covered, including primary liability, physical damage, passenger accident, and cargo insurance. Have several agents bid on your needs to get the best coverage at the appropriate rate.

Stay in Compliance - You will have many time-sensitive and filing requirements to apply for and submit. Failure to do any of these in an untimely manner may cost you good standing, delinquent fees, and perhaps even revoke your legal status of operation. Keeping your required reports, licenses, and permits all in order is a must; find a management system to help you stay on top of these and all document submissions in a timely fashion.

Finding Customers to Help You Grow Your Business - Though the use of load boards can get you immediate deliveries, and word of mouth works if you spend time conversing with many people, the best way to make money and have a thriving trucking company is to have a marketing strategy which is aimed at your audience. Learn the tools presented here, and you'll be a master at your own success for as long as you own your business.

Learn and Build a Marketing Strategy - You are in the right place to learn these techniques and design your path for a successful and profitable CDL operating company. But first things first. Before we begin with marketing methods and how you'll gain customers and business, some foundational concepts need to be in place in order for the strategies to make sense.

Trucking companies are unique in many ways. Our hours are different from most other businesses. We comply with federal regulations for times driving and time off. We have hours and hours of training and learning our rigs. We read, drive, listen, test, apply, and submit more paperwork than a college student applying for loans.

We drive in the day, we drive at night, we drive in the ice, sleet, rain, snow, and we drive in the fog. We even drive in temperatures over 100F degrees. We work up to 70 hours in an eight-day week, but have to make sure we don't drive longer than 11 hours straight. Most days we drive over 500 miles.

So what is so appealing about being a truck driver?

Well, each of us has our own definition and reason, but living the same lifestyle with other like-minded people who live by these standards brings comradery and understanding to the job. Some do it for life, some get in and get out, and some drivers never feel at home unless they are headed down the road to the unknown, stretched out and unforeseen, in front of them.

My point being, we are a different breed. We understand each other, though we know each of us is unique and different.

And then there are those of us who want to run a business.

We are, yet again, another segmented and divided group. But we have our ideas and we have our dreams. The first of which is to be our own boss.

You already know the trucking life and how it unfolds. Here, you will move from behind the wheel, frustrated, to being in front of your goals, which is success. Our industry is tough and not everyone could handle its ups and downs. But when you own your own trucking business, you are in charge and you are the boss.

Let's identify the areas which prove to be the most challenging in the CDL industry today, before beginning the marketing structure or methodology.

We'll outline several concerns and how to react, respond, and maneuver through these problems, so you can see how to identify the actual need, develop several ways to solve the problem, and then choose the best solution for your particular circumstance.

The trucking industry has been hit hard by environmental concerns, fluctuating fuel costs, driver shortages, trucking regulations, safety concerns, and now the COVID-19 pandemic. Each of these set-backs are out of the trucker's reach to solve. However, the best thing we can do is to be proactive and address each of them, depending on how closely they are related to your particular business.

Environmental Concerns - What can you do to lessen the impact of your driving on the environment? Make it part of your campaign if it's necessary to your customers. Also, be aware of your surroundings; people outside our circle are watching us carefully. Again, by being proactive, you can disarm confrontations, both direct and indirect, by recycling when possible, taking precautions with the environment, and being respectful of others' point of views.

Fluctuating Fuel Costs - Because the fuel industry has been pulled into politics and its roller coaster ride of power, being a business owner with a budget to predict is somewhat of a guessing game. If you can average on the higher side and still maintain a lucrative strategy, do it. If not, govern your best bet on the average cost over a period of time (2 years, 5 years, 10 years). This may be an area you will have to monitor closely. Keeping a prudent eye on the current costs can prevent losses down the road. And always buy fuel based on the cheapest *base price*, not pump price!

Driver Shortages - Hiring experienced drivers to work for you can be the most expensive challenge of your business. It can also give you the best rewards. If you have the time to hold out for the stellar drivers, of course, do. But often, independent drivers are hired to just get a commitment delivered to keep the customer. If possible, always keep the communication open with all drivers. If there is anyone who may know the good and bad points of a driver, it's a fellow driver.

Trucking Regulations and Toll Charges - There are several ways regulations and toll charges are calculated. As an operator, you need to be aware of these regulations before conducting charges for your services, as tolls and regulations change often, especially if you drive through more states or countries than your own. Passes are usually the easiest way to take care of business, but as you know, there are several places where weigh stations and individual tolls can be charged. Some charge by axle count, others by size of your rig, some even charge with a combination of the two, such as the New York State Thoroughfare. Stay up-to-date on these fees, particularly when quoting bids, and you will cover yourself when it comes time to pay up.

Safety Concerns - These are rules of the road and have steep penalties if not abided by. Being the owner, you are walking a fine line between taking care of your drivers and getting shipments delivered on time. Rule of thumb, always err on the safety of your driver and staying within restriction codes. They are there for a reason.

According to the Census of Fatal Occupational Injuries, 2019, heavy tractor-trailer truck drivers had the highest fatality rate (831 of 966 in Transportation Fatalities[3]) of any other occupation. Occupational Safety and Health Administration (OSHA) has strict regulations in place because of this consistent statistic, and others which are even more alarming, which rank CDL operators as *the highest risk occupation for injury*. Keep yourself and your drivers safe to the best of your abilities, as well as everyone else on the road; know the regulations and abide by them.

High Cost of Load Boards - There will always be the chance you will have an empty truck and need to go to a load board to find a load. But keep this practice to a minimum. Deal directly with the shipper whenever possible, as brokers retain anywhere from 10% to 25% of the load price. The obvious reason is very understandable, but remember, it costs you money in the long run.

COVID-19 - Transportation is always at the call of demand, and when revenues shut down, so does the trucking industry. Now is a hard time to begin a trucking company, but it's not impossible if you design your niche with knowledge. By planning well, choosing your developments wisely, and making sure you aren't over-spending or under-delivering, you will outlast the companies who are dropping their fundamentals to stay on the road. Keep to your commitment of your brand, your business image, and you will attract like-minded and CDL Minded customers that will appreciate your customer care and your honesty.

Because the trucking industry promises such plentiful business returns (profits), many have invested who know little about its personality. Putting together a smart and stable business plan then pursuing a savvy and responsive marketing strategy will not only serve you well in establishing yourself within the industry, but if done right, it will sustain you in the coming months and years.

All challenges are solvable; what looks big without knowledge becomes child's play when the secrets are known. Dig in and master the skills. The basis of developing a plan to move forward is to know what you are moving forward *with*.

In the next chapter you will learn how to develop a strategy for your company and the importance of having it in place.

CHAPTER TWO

The 9 Effective Necessities for Your Marketing Strategy

The hopes you have for your business carries great power when assembling your business plan and strategizing a marketing campaign.

This is only the beginning, however. Building a successful marketing strategy depends on mastering a few simple ideas. Namely, knowing exactly what your business focus is and who is your ideal customer. You need to be steadfast on the identity of your company and what you will offer before you can extend those services to customers and clients. Being clear doesn't mean being broad-minded, so narrow it down. Instead of saying 'We deliver farm-grown produce to local markets and independent grocers' try 'By specializing in organically farmed produce, our standards for delivery are as high as your standards are for growing.' By stating specifics, you draw in the customers who are passionate about their product. The more specialized the client's product, the more passionate they are about it, and they will try to do business with the same type of people.

What Market Are You Going to Provide Service To?

We've touched on this previously, but now you need to drill it down and decide exactly who your clients will be. If you are still wondering what industry you want to provide service to, or thinking you'll just open your doors and see who walks in, your marketing and any other investment to attain customers will be expensive and it will fail miserably. If you don't have a clear voice to speak directly to your client, they will never hear your message. If this is the case, chances are they will hear the message of your competitor.

Once you have determined the industry which will be your focus, you need to put yourself in your potential customers 'shoes' and discover who they are and what they are passionate about.

What Problems Do Your Customers Have?

Not only do you have to understand who they are and what they are passionate about, but you need to identify any needs, pains, or problems they may have. Imagine yourself as a business owner in their company. What would you be concerned with? What problems do you have that you wish would be solved?

By being the answer to their grief and problems, you will rise on a pedestal, and they will come to you time and time again.

So, if you've identified their needs and possible problems, where do you go from there?

Produce a marketing message which asks them about their problem. For example:

"Are you experiencing consistently late deliveries by your trucking firm?"

Then solve the problem:

"We guarantee every delivery is on time and on budget."

A guarantee is a binding promise, so remember, when solving their problem, don't over-commit. If you can't do it, don't say you can.

Maybe you could bring it down a notch:

"If a delivery is late, the next shipment is 50% off!"

Perhaps your potential customer has trouble finding trucks to deliver their product quickly, or perhaps they need pick-up times within 24 hours. You could advertise:

"Full fleet of delivery trucks to provide immediate pick-up."

If a client needs custom trailer packing because of delicate equipment, you could state:

"We offer on-site personal loading, to your specifications."

How Can You Solve Those Needs or Problems?

This is why you are in business; to help others and provide a product or service. You know these answers. It's why you have the desire to thrive in your own business. If you develop a strategy which will catch your customers' attention by identifying their problems, provide solutions to those problems, and make the process of getting that solution easy, effective, and productive, you are well on your way to building a clientele who will be loyal and engaging customers for life.

Now, let's get down to specifics. Here are the ways to get your marketing strategy moving forward.

9 Effective Necessities for Your Marketing Strategy

1) Stand out from your competition by portraying a unique business advantage in your niche.

You have your own style and way of doing things. Though each of us are different and handle situations uniquely, in business we are attracted to those who tend to think and approach our livelihoods similarly. In other words, we trust someone who we feel connected to intuitively rather than someone we don't quite understand or value.

Stay clear in your message and keep it simple. Don't be afraid to show your clients who you are and what your business stands for. Like-minded clients will notice and will be easier to win over.

There will always be people who don't see the world the same way as you. And this is fine, as you won't be able to please everyone all the time. Focus on the customers and clients who do matter, who do value your work ethic and appreciate what you have to offer. Keeping these companies well attended to and satisfied will keep you busy enough without worrying why another company didn't sign on with you. There are always wonderful customers out there who are looking for you and hoping you can help them with their needs.

2) Build a good, reliable reputation.

A good reputation is priceless and takes time to build. The sooner you show your business integrity and how you approach problems and solutions, the sooner you will establish yourself and develop credibility in your industry. Word spreads, especially if you turned a bad situation into a quick solution. Share your experiences in your marketing strategy too (on your website and as customer testimonials, discussed in further detail in Chapter 6). The more you show how dependable, trustworthy, and reliable you are, the quicker your customers will share their positive experiences, and your client base will grow at a lively pace.

Independent truck companies are at a disadvantage when it comes to public images. Yes, we are seen as being professional drivers and most people admire our skills and courtesy. But sometimes our good value gets lost in the race, and even we begin to question if we are capable of handling the stress or question if we are giving good service.

Take the initiative and be the best you can be. Self-respect is a big motivator and can get you through the darkest of times. When you work independently, we all know, you can come across hard times now and again. When you know you are doing a good job, the best job you can, and you are providing a great service to your customers and their businesses, you can cross insecurity and doubt right off the list.

And if you find yourself questioning your abilities or direction, realize where you are now doesn't necessarily mean you will be there next year, 5 years from now, or even at retirement age. You have the means to create greatness.

Stay away from temptations which can defeat your intentions. Keep a clean record free of drug, alcohol, or accident-related incidents. Pursue good routes, growth opportunities, and higher expectations from your business. By setting the bar just a bit higher, you can reach the goal and move toward the next one with more ease and incentive.

3) Maximize visibility.

Within the industry of CDL operators, there are thousands of different types of hauling. Using a multiple-faceted marketing strategy can help you reach all of your potential clients for your specific business. You may have clients who are on the internet for most of their day, while another client is on the phone or traveling between cities. To reach each of these potential clients, you must first determine where they spend their time, and, secondly, what marketing tool you need to use to best reach and communicate with each one.

The first and foremost hub of your market presence is to have a current and updated website. It's your calling card, information sheet, personal secretary, and talent list all rolled into one. In today's world, without one, you are invisible to your clients, without credibility and without information. You will find out how to launch the easiest of sites with the best information stated, announcing you are open and ready for business. Look to the later chapters to achieve this task, and no, it really isn't as daunting as it sounds.

Make sure your image comes off in a professional manner also. Being a professional entrepreneur takes strength and agility, not to mention patience and diligence. By showing you are a business owner who commands all these traits, you will draw the same level of professionalism in your clientele. You won't be dealing with hustlers or companies who undercut your bids or devalue your service. By portraying the image of a business professional you want to work with, you will attract and retain great customers and like-minded, responsible companies. No one wants to work with half-rate businesses and agents who don't 'deliver' on what they promise.

4) Develop customer relationships.

As much as this seems like a given, more often than not business own-ers get caught up in the day-to-day operations and fail to acknowledge their potential and existing customers. When building your client base, take more time to get to know the people who are reading your website, answering your posts, commenting on your social media, or asking questions on the phone. Become interested in them, and they will see you in a different and positive light.

Your existing clients need attention in this way too. Keep them feeling like they are as important five years down the road as they were the day they signed their first contract. Stay engaged, ask about new directions they are taking and how you can make the process easier for them. Each client will handle the communication differently, so having several avenues to connect (email, messaging, phone calls, etc.) provides a better chance for keeping and maintaining a great rela-tionship with them. By offering many ways to connect, you are also making it easier for them to be in touch with you, as well as providing more opportunity for the relationship to develop with trust and loyalty.

Also, take care to keep the lines of communication open, and always welcome their input and views. Even if you have a client who seems like they don't wish to speak with you, stay in contact. Send them your newsletter once a month or keep them on your promotions list to receive your latest discounts. You never know when they will need you, which may depend on either a rush transport across town, or an emergency haul across the country. If you are on their radar when the moment arises, chances are they will give you a try. Just because you don't hear from a customer doesn't mean they aren't listening.

5) Maintain a level playing field, whether you are a large company or a single-person operation.

In today's marketing world, you can be large or small, specific or broad. By strategizing your marketing to reach your specific customers and give them exactly what they are in need of, you have accomplished the main objective. Do you have to knock on a million doors to land that one big account?

No, all you have to do is find out where they 'are' (interests, commonalities, demographics), why they are there, and create relatable messaging to 'speak' to them personally. Your image can be as big or as small as you choose, especially when conversing online. The internet gives you any number of ways to project your brand and gain trust. If done correctly, you can win out over large competition, time and time again, by focusing your personal service, offering customized care, and building an engaged network.

You also offer something the large companies and corporations can't offer, and that is 'the personal touch.' If a client feels they have your attention and is confident you will do everything in your power to get them what they need, they will return this customized attention back to you with continued business and word-of-mouth praise.

Large companies may offer customer service or have staff waiting at the end of a phone line to take calls, but what a business owner who is having you move their product wants is to know how that person views their product, will safety for their shipment be at risk, or will the driver be rude to the receiving dock, who you know, is a bit of a *tough old dog*. You already know, the large companies do have their great drivers, some of them have all great drivers. But as a client in a large pool of businesses, it is pretty much a given that you won't have the same driver each time, and you won't be able to connect with them like you can with the customized and care-driven trucking business.

Never underestimate the power of being a personalized and helpful operator. Everyone wants to know someone has their back and won't shortcut their promise. Large companies don't neglect their customers intentionally, but at some point their customers do feel like they are just a number in the system. And that suits many businesses, but these aren't your customers; this isn't the world where you will shine.

We all would much rather have a personal connection with our business partners than be an order number at the end of the day. Take advantage of this, listen to your customer, ask questions to make sure you understand their business and their needs. Then deliver the best possible service you can provide, all with a couple of preliminary conversations and a sincere 'thank you' after the job is completed. There isn't a bad or weak spot in this scenario at all. By being an attentive and supportive supplier, you will possess their devotion time and time again.

5) Achieve a high return on your investment.

In today's marketing world, you can spend hundreds and thousands of dollars on marketing techniques and ad campaigns. But, you can also spend your dollars wisely (or take advantage of many directives which are free or cost next to nothing to use) and attain just as much as those expensive and hit-and-miss blanket campaigns.

By focusing on a specific niche, industry, product, or service, you can get the attention of your intended audience easily, make your offer, and gain new business quickly and easily, all while doing what comes easiest for you and providing exactly the service needed for your customer. Your potential clients are intelligent and savvy; they know what they want and when they see you offer that exact thing, they will engage with you quickly and become faithful followers. The power of placing yourself in front of their eyes has never been easier, and creating a brand and presence in the places where your clients will be found can be inexpensive and lucrative.

In addition to narrowing down your audience target to the exact audience you want as ideal customers, it's wise to offer them more value than what they initially want. By being the best business owner you can be, you will give them the confidence of knowing you are top-notch in every area of your industry. This includes:

- Being current and up-to-date on your permits, licenses, insurance, and regulations.

- Always looking for innovative and cost-effective ways to save money, not only for your business, but for your customer too.

- Staying current and possibly even a leader in furthering your education; this gives you the knowledge you'll need to incorporate new techniques into your business.

- Have back-up plans in case of emergencies and keep a watchful eye on economic downturns by evaluating the effect they may have on your industry and business.

- Always be aware of your competition's strategies and tactics; stay one step ahead of them with your own techniques and offers if possible.

In other words, be the exceptional operator.

When you know what is going on in the world around you, you can speculate, plan, and prepare for good and bad times, and you will have the satisfaction and knowledge that you will always be there for your company and its success, as well as your customers and their ever-changing needs.

6) Lower marketing and operating costs.

Your own sector of industry, or niche, can give you many options to reach your clients, and quite often they are very specific. Online advertising can give you the options you want at minimal costs, sometimes even free!

Maybe you are a milk tanker line, and you are trying to reach independent dairies. How do you reach those rural people with your company benefits of 24/7 hourly truck availability or scheduled routine customized routes for the latest in dairy transport?

First, where are these dairy farmers in terms of managing their own business? Most currently have multiple dairies and many employees, and being small as a single dairy farmer just isn't feasible any longer. Where is the decision maker to be found? They probably check the price of goods each day (online, which means you might want to run a banner ad on popular investment sites) or perhaps merchandise which the farmer may need (a banner ad on milking machine sites or bovine vet care). Many of these ads can be set up as a rotating ad, and you only pay for each 'click' or time a person checks out your page or site (pay per click, or PPC). Today's options couldn't align better with the small business CDL trucker.

Can you see how and where your money will do the most good? When you use an approach of segment influence, you can reach even the most elusive of customers. As you become more educated about your niche, you'll also be able to see how analysis reports will give you the answers you are in need of when a campaign doesn't quite give you what you were looking for, or what words will turn a warm response to your ad into an explosive one.

It's also a good idea to stay up on your driving requirements and keep a clean record. By being in good standing with all the agencies, state, and federal mandates, it shows that you're responsible and you handle your business in a professional manner. These things are vitally important to customers. If you have savvy and responsible customers yourself, as you are hoping to acquire, they will check to make sure your business is an operation that they'll want to transport their goods. If you have a poor standing within your industry, your potential customers will find someone else to move their product.

7) Establish yourself as an innovator.

Chances are, one of the reasons you want to own your own business is that you want to improve something or offer an alternative. You've taken the first step, but don't stop there.

By showing your ability to adapt, to handle emergencies, and to move forward with smart solutions and ideas, you will also catch the attention of customers and build rapport as a company which can handle the tough stuff. There are so many ways a CDL operator can be tripped up by outside forces. Show your customers you can handle yourself under pressure, and you've won their faith for unexpected but inevitable challenges.

Always keep up on trends and changes in the industry too. If there is a way to improve driving techniques or expand the services you offer, evaluate the options and see if they may benefit you.

Along the way of keeping up-to-date, employing changes to stay on top of your business, and showing professionalism in stressful times, make sure you recognize yourself for the valuable and resourceful person that you are. Without initiative, without incentive, and without applied knowledge, your business would fold in the turn of a wheel. Your self-worth and confidence is what keeps your business making money and your truck(s) on the road. Congratulate yourself for the steps you've taken to get to your higher ground. No one else could have done this quite like you have—be proud of your achievements and motivation.

8) Initiate, communicate, listen, and engage.

Always remember to take advantage of connecting with potential and established customers. In today's world, everyone is accustomed to being social and having acquaintances. 'Likes' are valued on Facebook just as much as the number of connections on LinkedIn. It is also very demanding. If we don't like what we are seeing or who we are working with, we simply detach and find another outlet.

Your business will be no different. If someone is feeling abandoned or neglected (and it probably will happen over the lifetime of your company), they will take their marbles and leave the game. On the other hand, you may very well be the game they decide to join if disappointments have occurred with another company. Even if you aren't the 'chatty' type, find someone who is and put them in charge of your customer relations. Establishing and maintaining a vigilant connection, whether your clients answer back or not is essential to running and building a successful business in today's world.

Always be there to answer questions and offer help. Make sure you communicate within a business day's passing, if only to say you are away from your desk but will be back in touch when you are able. If you don't know the answer, don't pretend that you do. Nothing shows worse than someone trying to be something they aren't. Tell them you don't know, but you will find the answer and be right back with them. This lets them cross the issue off their to-do list and gives you an opportunity to not only come to their rescue, but you show humility and the initiative to learn. By being a good partner to them when they ask, you show your customer you will be there when needed.

Just as you are when you're purchasing a product or service yourself, all the customer wants is:

- to be listened to and appreciated

- to have their need or promise fulfilled

When you engage with your customer, you are giving them the respect and attention they are looking for, while at the same time, showing your dignity and integrity for them and your business. These attributes will set you apart in your industry.

9) Be flexible.

It's fair to say, sometimes your strategy will go right out the window and the effects of an event will leave you with a quiet phone and an empty inbox. Don't take it personally. For every lost customer, there are ten who can't wait to have you haul for them.

Though these situations are hopefully few and far between, they do happen, and when they do, the best game plan is to adjust your sails, catch a breeze (or in our case a road), and head in a more viable direction.

The pandemic has brought chaos to the most sound of industries, leaving over 14 million people in America unemployed. It has upended many companies in the CDL trucking industry, while at the same time overburdened others.

Some trucking companies don't have enough hours in the day; consider an operator delivering groceries and food items, or another transporting medical supplies. Their industries have been moving non-stop for months, and it is likely to become overly busy again if case numbers continue to climb. For those transporting fuel or supply parts to manufacturers, it's anything but busy.

As manufacturing production dropped, so did truckers' schedules. Needs for parts and components dwindled, and as the pandemic spread and states restricted travel, so did the dynamic of the CDL industry.

A key indicator to the downturn of our industry is recognized on spot market rates and load boards. It represents close to 20% of the industry, pairing companies which need a load shipped and truckers looking for a load to fill their return or original trips.

Since March 2020, the overall number of available loads posted were up 39.1% compared to the previous year, while the increase in trucks looking for loads increased by 6.3%. As March drew to a close, however, the last week of March in particular, spot load posts dropped 38.7%, while trucks looking for loads increased to 12.7%.

The new turn? Truckers are having to hustle to find freight their trucks can move. The trucking industry wasn't part of the relief in the CARES Act (Coronavirus Aid, Relief, and Economic Security) but many companies are looking for Small Business Administration program relief for payroll and loans. Everything else is an innovative hustle for truckers who are in need of moving freight and completing runs. Though many large companies have donated funding to help keep the trucking industry afloat—Goodyear Tire & Rubber Company as well as Convoy Freight Network, for example—trucking companies are still struggling to keep their trucks running and their drivers busy.

In addition to the pandemic and the troubles it has caused, driver distraction incidents have almost doubled since this time in 2019. It could be related to a lower perceived need to focus due to the decrease in traffic on the road, or drivers under mounting stress from income decreases or health issues. Whatever the cause, the trucking industry is, once again, having to jump unseen hurdles and overcome building grief.

When considering, however, the smaller trucking business, who has 2 to 3 trucks to run and 10 to 20 customers to service, how does this scenario play out for them? No data was found, as these businesses are usually solely owned, and would most likely have to apply for any help through the Small Business Administration as did their larger counterparts. But when a small business misses 5 loads and 10 billing tickets, it is a devastating blow. Most often they can't get a piece of the available action either, due to the network of larger companies and alliances shared from within.

You, However, Are Different

With all of these facts and details affecting the small business opera-tor, though, there is hope in the belief we will survive. Make no mis-take, we will struggle and have our own share of faulty records or sick drivers. But one thing is clear. We are a feisty lot, and when one thing doesn't work, we back up and try another route.

You as a new or established business owner, will also learn how to do this, if you haven't figured it out already. Because you have seen choosing a niche can change, even in the slightest way, to create a new client base, you can evaluate new possibilities for your business and provide service to new clientele. By having the ability to create oppor-tunities and the knowledge to adjust for changes, you will come out as a winner, banged up a bit, maybe, but never beaten.

With the knowledge this book provides, you will not only be able to change course and adjust to the new options if necessary, you will create new methods to attract the attention of your desired customers, with just the right offer at just the right time.

Remember, all your client wants is to be listened to and have their needs met; you do this for them, and you will have a loyal client for life. There are more ways to create a marketing campaign than there are stars in the sky; start small, think big, know the strategy inside and out, and expand to other ideas which link to your foundational strategy to grow your brand and your client base.

Using proven methods in the beginning can give you ideas on how to adapt the basics to your specific needs. In the next chapter you will learn how to map out your strategy in a meaningful and progres-sive manner.

CHAPTER THREE

Covering All the Bases

Remember when we said knowing your business objectives inside and out will give you a strong foundation on which to build your business? Well, here is where that comes into play. You know your direction, now you get to choose the tools to build your path to success.

Within marketing or advertising, you have an incredible number of avenues you can take to get your company recognized. Certain methods can utilize specific products—services may be presented better in one light than in another—and some techniques just make it easier to achieve higher sales than others.

To learn the complete strategies of marketing and the subtleties of doing one tactic and then another, people have attained degrees, written manuscripts, conducted statistical analysis, and tried many other noteworthy methods of acquiring knowledge and mastering skills. This path takes time, energy, and money, few endeavors any of us want to commit to.

Truth be told, all you have to do is know what you want your company to excel in, create this image when marketing and branding your business, and drill down to discover who your target audience is.

That's it.

Everything else is just choice and application.

Choose the result you want, work your way backward to the beginning, and see what path will get you to the goals you want to reach. By starting your marketing thought process with these simple ideas, you can get the answers you are looking for. Most business owners need multiple campaigns to figure out this simple process!

Traditional Advertising

Television ads, both local and national, cable, internet, and digital - Production of television ads can run from thousands to millions of dollars. Sometimes, if you can specifically target your idea audience on TV, then the money spent to run the ad may be worth it. If you only want a local reach, say for delivering business packages to a neighborhood pharmacy, you can purchase 'ad packages' which target a specific area. Production for your ad (or video) should also be prudent, as spending a lot of money on a commercial can easily happen when things don't go smoothly and resources have to be tapped to make it all work. Schedules put together to 'run' your ads can be expensive also, so a brief budget analysis might be a good idea to determine before you start taking videos of your crew in action.

Radio ads, broadcast and Internet - Producing a radio spot by yourself can be very economical, especially if you believe you'll be using this kind of marketing for a longer period of time, such as using audio podcasts for example. Investing in recording equipment and software can be pricey, but good devices which will serve you well can be set up for about the same price as a first run campaign. You can also use your audio recordings on other media, such as Instagram or Facebook. Many radio stations also have recording studios available to use if you want top-notch recordings for a nominal price. Talent can also be hired for production of your ads too.

Advertising on vehicles, cars, buses, etc. - With the innovation of 'wrapping,' vehicle advertising has become quite a lucrative business. For a price, you can get your message put on a vehicle which will be on the road for a designated amount of time. Buses are another alternative, and use plastic poster boards for their advertising, which has proven to be a good choice, offering many great options for print production. You will usually be locked into a longer period of time for your ad, so be strategic. Don't choose a specific promotion which you'll have to honor for longer than you can either afford or want to offer.

Industry-specific periodicals (online and hard copy) ad, article, op-ed – Targeting a specific audience can sometimes be frustrating. While advertising in a periodical or newspaper most often will be broad, it can give you some nuggets of good contact if your potential customer is tied into the same focus as your business, such as transporting thoroughbred horses. Look at the description of the publication on its website and see if it aligns with your intent.

Writing articles, guest blogs, and opinion editorials for magazines and/or popular blogs can also bring you notoriety and get your business' name out into view. If you do write, make sure your article is of interest and is written well. Make sure the grammar is proper and spelling has been checked, maybe with Google Drive or Grammarly. Considering these are free options, the advantages are endless. You could also put the same article on your LinkedIn Profile, a Facebook page for your business, and a blog post on your website. By linking the keywords and your business, the search engines will recognize your article and give it a higher preference ranking each time it's viewed, the more the better.

Purchasing a booth at trade shows, conferences - Though targeting an audience at these types of events can be fairly easy and specific, considerations need to be weighed, as these shows and conferences often draw large and diverse crowds with little else in common other than the topic at hand. Shows can be broad in attraction or very specific, such as outdoor supply retailers. You may be looking at this exact type of marketing, and if so, heed caution. This type of marketing tool is generally very expensive, not only for the space you occupy (your booth), but also the man-hours spent in planning the event, transportation and housing for hosts and booth, and additional fees tied into display and advertising of your booth (sometimes union fees, electrical needs, optional advertising packages, and set up/take down costs).

The most successful trade show exhibits are usually large companies who can dominate the trade show floor, or at least compete in it. The smaller participants most often are lost in the large crowds.

As an attendee, however, you can gleen quite a bit of information about an industry and its influences at these types of shows, and your competitors.

UPDATE: As of March 2020, most trade shows have been indefinitely postponed due to the COVID-19 pandemic. Check on industry websites and reviews for current standings and dates. If you are thinking of this niche for your company, do your homework. It's believed this industry will return, but what it will look like after the pandemic is anyone's guess.

Outdoor advertising (billboards, sporting event sponsorship, building wraps, etc.) – The sponsorships for sporting events is a very broad audience and wouldn't be prudent for many businesses. The same can be said for billboards, although if you are strictly working in local transport or logistics this could serve you well. They are a bit on the expensive side and usually run a month at a time. Again, weigh the benefits and judge accordingly for length of exposure.

Media blitz (sponsorship of a business promo, sport team, charity event, etc.) – Having an event at your place of business with a radio sponsorship broadcasting can be costly, but if executed properly, it can serve you well for quite some time, as people can have a delayed response. Usually, it's conducted as an Open House, but can be advertised with any promotion you believe may work. A word of caution: most often, media blitzes take some time to make up for their initial costs. You'll pay upfront for the radio or channel televised, which often includes a 'personality' talent fee, refreshments for everyone involved, including your team who's supporting the media, and any promotions you feel necessary for its success.

Online Advertising

Business website – As time passes, having an active and informative website is becoming as necessary as having a name. You can get business from generic searches (this is called organic response), possible engagement when the keywords you use on your website puts your name at the top of a search page, and business when a past client wants to use your services again, but can't spell your name right. All this and more is tied to having a website. More than 3.8 million searches per minute are handled by Google alone (January 2020), and to miss out on this chunk of business is like giving your competitor the password to your bank account.

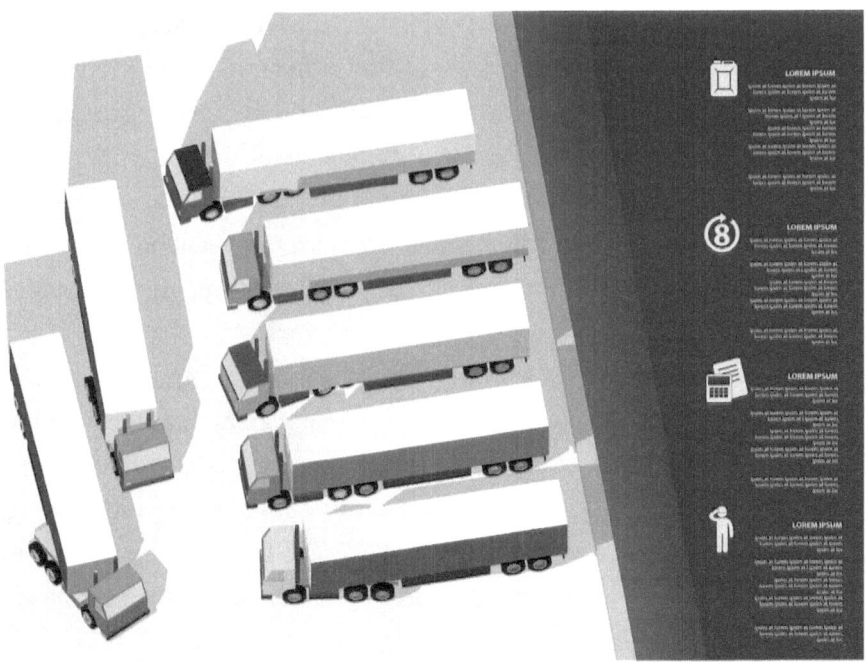

Company blog and posts - Keep your customers updated on changes and improvements, offer them discounts or bonuses with promotions during slow times, or just have a place where drivers can share. When you connect yourself and your company image to others on a more intimate basis than a handshake, an invoice, and a check, you begin to develop relationships which can grow and thrive; it's what businesses in these device-driven times thrive on.

You can also develop a following, which looks for your regular posts and is eager to support your endeavors and challenges. Consider this the replacement of a lunch and a handshake. Most days in our busy lives we don't have time to connect personally, but by sharing industry information and support, you can build networks which are stronger and have more people involved than you ever imagined. And this, in turn, brings strength and continuity to your company today and in the future.

Industry-specific blog (opinion articles, thoughts) - By writing industry-specific news articles, overcoming a common obstacle or sharing an experience you've had which you think others may find interesting, you will make your company more 'personable' and more approachable. People see you as a person when you share yourself and your ideas, and this is one of the most important things in developing and retaining client relations. In an age where devices govern our availability, making any part of those experiences more human will win over almost anyone.

Social media accounts (like a mini-website, Pinterest, Instagram, etc.) - Many apps can create an account and post items which are relevant to the creator's directives, both stagnant (a picture or PDF) and moveable (a video or phone clip). If you are a photographer, Instagram lets you post as many of your own images as you care to, with the option to 'promote' certain pictures for marketing or social connecting purposes. Pinterest is much the same.

If you choose to create a presence in any of these social media apps, read up on the basics at the website home page so you understand their rules and guidelines. If you stray from these social media's preferences, their internal algorithms will dismiss your account and postings, and it won't matter how often you log on and post content. If you are breaking the rules from the start, you will be at the bottom of the scrolling vacuum.

Most often, YouTube has incredible information in an easy-to-understand format for posting and promoting on these sites. There are also countless offers for software programs to help you navigate. You may want to save these channels for later, when you feel comfortable with your online brand and your website is running smooth.

Social media ads (Facebook, YouTube, Google, LinkedIn, etc.), can be an automated ad, video, standing link, or giveaway via email address - Once you become familiar with online sites such as Facebook, Google, and LinkedIn, you'll begin to notice the scrolling offers on the side and at the top of the pages you search. The way these recurring ads appear are devised through the now famous process of applying 'cookies,' small 'markers' which remember what you've done in the past, so they can recall and expose you to it again in the future. These can benefit an advertiser, but they can also send your paid-in-advance marketing plan into the dark reaches of cyber no-man's-land, so make sure you have your keywords and key phrases in place to 'land' on the site's appropriate page(s).

When you understand what a site offers as an advertising vehicle, you can make sure your ad abides by the 'cookies' rules and doesn't get tossed aside. You'll also need to keep an eye on your ads to make sure this doesn't happen. No one will notify you if your ads aren't making it to viewing pages. One last note: determine a budget and stick to it. Don't fall for the 'one more week' ad campaign. If it's not bringing you the numbers you are looking for, pull it, rework it, and post again for another round for viewing.

Affiliate marketing promotions (sales from a 'partner' who leads the customer to you) - This can be a very lucrative way to not only connect with industry-driven people, but you can make money and share abiding customers with other vendors you believe your clients would enjoy. It works like this: you both agree to promote a particular product or service, one of which is the originator of the item and finalizes the sale, and the other is the 'affiliate' who promotes the item to their client list and receives a percentage of any sale. It can also be a great way to share clients if you have businesses which support each other, say a vendor and a shipper combine a promotion to offer to both their client lists and split profits. Some also call these 'joint ventures.'

Webinars selling programs or group offers – If you feel comfortable in front of a camera, maybe you would like to share a particular favorite ride you do often, or want to discuss a topic of interest to several people you sell services to. Maybe you can show how to install a sound system in the cab, how to keep refrigerators and freezers performing at optimal levels (in static locations or as trailers), or how to perform specific services on your truck/trailer.

Article publication promotions (opinion article on an industry website) – If you wanted to share your particular experience with a vendor or business you like, writing an article or posting an opinion piece on their website is also a great way to get your name out and tie your business with another you admire. Sometimes you can do this openly, other companies request you have permission before posting information. Industry websites can be incredibly resourceful and offer clients and customers from places you had no idea how to reach. There are many clubs set up around small businesses and entrepreneurs, which also offer guidance and conversation between colleagues. Volunteer an article or two, and pretty soon you will get referrals from people who will like what you have to say.

PPC (pay per click) you only pay for 'clicks' of interests for an ad or promotion – As mentioned before, PPC can be beneficial if you want people to go to a specific page or place on your website. If you are promoting a special or want to share something specific, this is a great avenue to use. Many companies swear by PPC, and others have found it to be cumbersome. Do some investigating on your own; cruise through some of your favorite retail pages. Notice the ads running on the side and see if you can spot the PPC advertisers. Common characteristics are large retailer websites who are looking to sell side space on their site, such as DIY retail stores or large investment firms. The little ads change often, and usually ask for your email first, so they can send you future promotions. A local trucking company could make a lucrative business from running PPC campaigns on a local large outlet store. If you are in a long-haul business design, however, you may want to bypass this option, unless you see a perfect way to utilize the process.

A Mix of Traditional and Online Marketing

Multimedia marketing campaigns - A well-rounded marketing strategy will get you maximum exposure while narrowing in on the avenues of advertising you feel are best for your particular customer. Having a website with a blog up and running with supportive flyers posted in coffee shops or restaurants can cover a broad range of clientele without spending too much money on your efforts.

If a billboard will support your online reach and interaction, then by all means, go ahead and see where it lands. Listen to your heart, dig around to see if your ideal client profile would likely see or interact with your ads, and judge your outcomes. If the initial campaign doesn't produce success—and most likely while you are in the beginning stages, the successes may be sparse—change **one** characteristic and try it again. After you get results from that, compare it to the original and judge your outcome. Then, change another one, and run it again.

What you are doing is called 'A/B Testing' and you are comparing the first outcome to another by changing just one factor each time. It can also work well for engagement and comments on your blog or a particular promotion's draw of customers. When you combine the best of both traditional and online marketing, you set yourself up for recognition and success.

There is no single formula for a great advertising campaign - And even if there was a single GREAT formula, it would change tomorrow, just as your clients' needs change and the aspects of your business change; though, of course, there are some basics which can be used as good guidelines.

Being adaptable and learning to adjust quickly benefits everyone. It will prove well for your company to be able to recognize a poor choice and adjust for the better. It will show clients you are aware of current trends within your industry and adapt to the needed changes quickly, and it will look great on your financial statement—even as poor responses—when turned around quickly. It will be just a bump in the road instead of a major deficit disaster which looms longer than it should. Keep analyzing your results, adjust and tweek what you can, and move forward with expectations that what works today doesn't necessarily mean you're done with your marketing for the year.

The selection of the right approaches will depend on what you're trying to do and who you want to reach (where your customer is) - Know what's available to you and judge how each tool could affect your outcome. It's just like building a table; if you have a plan and use the right equipment and supplies, it can turn out beautiful. Choose the wrong tool or a weak piece of material, and the whole thing can fall in on itself. There are many options to choose from.

A combined approach employing the best of each - Depending on the direction you want your brand to take and the targeted audience you are after, having a varied plan will serve you and your ideal customer the best. Pick and choose a few foundational marketing approaches, such as an updated website design with committed blog posts, an Instagram journal of your travels, and a thank-you card sent to all new customers. Master these tools first and get to know them well, then change up a couple of things, add some new ideas to the journal or remove something which is cumbersome or hasn't received any response, and launch again. Try a promotion, change the colors on the website, word some key elements differently, each separate, and each monitored. You'll be a pro at marketing in no time, and have a dependable and stable business foundation to build your growth.

Innovative Marketing Approaches

At this point, you may be feeling a bit overwhelmed and that you may not have the skills or time to design a marketing campaign, nor the money to pay someone else to do it.

Rest assured, there are as many ways to get your company in the online sector of your niche as there are strategies to play poker. The importance of having a website, online blog, and an online journal are immense, but going online with these tools is as easy as watching a YouTube video. There are many common questions we all have when designing a website, putting together a video, or promoting your business on Facebook.

Writing effectively, for instance, comes with practice and mastering this skill will improve over time, whether it's writing an article for your blog or stating your mission statement. When you see something you like, notice the way the words are used and how they are set up to catch your attention. How did it catch your attention and can you incorporate a few items to initiate the same results for your marketing?

Noticing the things which get you in the mind frame of purchasing is the answer to developing your ideal marketing strategy. Before too long, you will master these skills and propel your company into the profits column. If you are doubting your ability to dissect another company's marketing strategy, fear not; the basics of assembling your marketing strategy and learning the secrets which will make the process easy will be shared with you in Step 1.

I feel intimidated by designing my own website, how can I write an ad?

It can't be stressed enough how important it is to have an online presence in the CDL business world today. Most of us connect with a handheld device, and when someone is in need of help, it's the first thing we reach for. It's one of the choices that your potential client reaches for when in need is crucial. If you have the answers to the problem, you are just a touch of a button away to have a customer call and get details. Make sure when you launch that your site looks good on all device faces, not just a computer.

Your website is not only a 'phone listing' of sorts for your potential clients, but it also acts as a bulletin board, an online store, an update notifier, and, most importantly, a connection to your established and potential customers. When used to even a fraction of its potential, a good website will give you a thousand times back in advantages and resolve what will possibly cost in time and effort spent initially to design and launch.

If you are stopped in your tracks at this point, get someone to put a site together for you. Don't let your own insecurities stop you from 'opening shop.' If nothing more, just get a landing page (WIX is easy to use and free) with your company name, a brief description of what you offer (hopefully a promotion, keep it small but descriptive so you'll know when someone has seen it and contacts you), contact information, and a place for them to leave a message (which will drop into your email box).

Even these simple actions will get you out there and online, and build your confidence. From there, you will be surprised at how easy it is to expand into more depth and opportunities to show off your business. Here are a few terms which you may or may not be familiar with, and where they will fit into your marketing strategy.

What is SEO and why do I need to know it?

SEO, or search engine optimization, is a fancy term for what Google or any other search engine does when it lists websites in order of popularity; it takes the words you enter into the search bar and delivers the most relevant answers, or the ones with the word(s) used the most or in the same order as your search.

The more people click on a site (or pay money to have it listed first), the higher it is listed on the results of a 'search' (when you type in a subject you want more information on or to connect to). The search engine uses 'keywords' or 'key phrases' to find what you are looking for and gives you the most relevant results by using integrated algorithms. If you are a CDL operator who hauls flowers for florists, you would want to put the keywords *flowers, florists, fresh, refrigerated, overnight delivery,* etc., into the descriptions of your pages, website, and offers. By having those in specific places on your site (such as in the headings and body text), you will catch the attention of Google, Bing, etc., and they will list your site in the results of potential clients looking for a way to get their roses to the coast.

What are the advantages of having a social media presence?

Having your company's name and identity on social media platforms such as Facebook, Instagram, and Pinterest can generate interest without you even being there. And it can be free.

Let's say you have a Facebook page for Trucker XYZ. Before you begin a trip you write a little note about what will make this trip special "Heading to St. Louis today and while I was mapping the trip, I noticed there is a Hoedown Roundup in Kansas City. Here's to all the cowboys riding those broncos!" with maybe a picture of the poster, a county fair pic, or maybe a cowboy with his horse.

Simple.

Easy.

When you get experienced enough, you'll be able to link this post to your other social media pages and create 'likes' and 'looks,' maybe even some favorites and followers who find things in common with your post.

The main point here is that you are getting your company name out there. When someone 'follows' you, it kicks back to others who follow them, and they check out your page. At some point, your post can connect to a potential customer who may need you in the future, so they save your link on their list or begin to follow your posted content.

This is the power of social media, and why you not only hear so much about it, but also need to get involved with it as soon as you feel comfortable, preferably right after you launch your website!

Is listing my business in a 'niche' industry directory profitable?

Directories have been in marketing since the concept was born, and they will always have a presence in a marketing campaign. Some industry directories are more prevalent than others, depending on the personality of the industry, but for the most part, if a directory has been publishing its services for more than 5 years, it is probably still a very viable tool for the niche. Because they are delivered as an electronic file now, it is easier than ever to use them in cold contact campaigns too.

There are many ways to use a directory, anything from announcing a new promotion or delivery location to surveying potential and established client opinions. Your creativity can play a huge part when using directories, especially if you have invested quite a large portion of your budget into it. But yes, many of them can be quite expensive depending on your niche and the number of contacts you are buying.

Should I be advertising on Yelp, Google My Business, Bing Places, Foursquare, and other local online business directories?

Local citations, an SEO result which uses locations as a key factor in pulling results, have now taken searching for nearby attractions by storm. With more and more people using their GPS and navigation apps to find the nearest malt shop or how many miles it is to Winnimuka, local citations are gaining incredible weight with potential clients and customers. By having your company listed in these, particularly the ones which are more specific to CDL operations, you could be the #1 listing if someone needs to get items delivered across town or across the nation. An added advantage, if you retain a local client, it gives you advantages of keeping in touch with them on a more intimate basis, such as discussing local sports or a favorite restaurant. By having local commonalities with your customer, you can engage in ways you aren't able to with customers in other cities. It's just one more avenue to 'share' while developing your network relations with your clients.

What are PPC promotions and how would they benefit my company?

PPC is an abbreviation for pay-per-click, as we've mentioned, and is quite a simple process. If you find a website you feel your audience would connect with often, you may want to advertise on the site to grab the attention of potential customers. Many sites who draw large numbers of viewers offer PPC ads, and will sell you a rotating ad space for a very reasonable price. You are only charged for each time someone 'clicks' on your ad to view more information, which is most often linked to a landing page or promotion offered in the ad.

Clicks can run from pennies per click to dollars per click. Generally, your ad needs to benefit the host site in some way also, either by being relevant to their product, service, or subject matter, or relates to their viewers in a fairly direct way. It is an attractive way of advertising without spending a lot on your promotion. By doing your homework with analytical numbers and seeing where your clicks are coming from, you can drill down on your audience fairly quickly, and it makes it a great tool to narrow the personality of your ideal client.

I hear the term 'content marketing' often; what is it and why is it important?

Content marketing is a form of marketing which uses integral methods—such as blogging, uploading videos, or making social media posts—to promote, publish, and distribute messaging to specific audiences. By using several different media tools, a message using the same wording in all marketing methods can be marketed to similar or different audiences to produce a blanket effect of a focused advertising concept.

When we use one idea and promote it in several different ways, we create a multiple tool effect to distribute a promotion throughout a larger group. A promotion will reach many people with the same message, despite them receiving the message through one particular marketing tool or another. Your business image is focused in one direction, so you don't sell multiple ideas to overlapping audiences.

The more cohesive of a campaign you have, the better the chances are of its success.

Content marketing has become a popular concept, and was originally driven into development due to the software advantages of analysis programs. Any analysis is redundant if it doesn't compare the same concept between subjects, so campaigns began a more singular focus and created the overall concept of content marketing. A wonderful side note: the more you use it, the more it solidifies your company's marketing brand.

I keep on seeing more and more YouTube and video ads online; is this a viable means of advertising?

Business owners, publishers, and online course distributors are all moving into video promotions as their number one sales promotion to use. Even retail stores and shops are developing new ways of bringing their products to your online device via video. From demonstrations on how to decorate cupcakes to showing the steps of installing a carburetor, businesses are discovering the easy, affordable, and readily accepted form of video for their marketing campaign.

This doesn't mean you personally have to get in front of your phone and video your discount or trailer loading policies. What you can do, however, is use a video to grab the attention of a possible viewer by panning a horizon of one of your hauls and dropping in a few lines of promotion for a PPC ad, showing how to clear foggy lenses on the road, or your latest opinion of a mapping app. Whatever you want to create conversations on, you can do a video to begin the dialogue.

Depending on how serious you want to be with your filming skills, you can use your phone for an off-the-cuff ad or spend thousands of dollars for a professional grade production. Whatever your choice, there's an acceptable, good process to use, and just about anything is useful when you post it in an ad.

One rule of the marketing world which goes without any argument: your audio needs to be great. Even if the picture is too light or the words can't be read well over a background, if the audio is good, people will move along with your message and not be distracted by the lesser quality of another portion.

But if the audio is poor, you will lose their attention immediately, and in this age of point and click, you'll be dismissed without even a second thought or glance. Invest in a good recording of the audio, don't sound like you're in a barrel, and you'll be set for the video portion of your marketing campaign.

As we move forward in putting your effective and easily assembled marketing strategy together, we'll focus on the 3-Step System of Building Your Business.

In Step 1, specifics will be discussed to determine your audience in all the aspects of your business plan, from identifying your loyal customers to finding the right drivers for you and your company. You'll key into the workings of your specific marketed customers, figuring out what their problems are, the problems they need solved, and how to remedy their troubles with your solutions. You'll also learn how to uncover the clients your competition has been overlooking, making you the star for initiating a connection, helping them solve their problems, such as increasing their client satisfaction or profit margin.

Step 2 will show you how to attain and keep your best customers, without wasting time with clients who will drain your energy and give you zeros in your profit margin. Budgets, costs of marketing, tips for advantages to your specific needs, and loyalty will give you an edge for attracting great clients and keeping them enthusiastic about working with you and, in a roundabout way, for you.

As briefly talked about earlier, Step 3 begins the process, showing you the steps to take in order to build your customized marketing strategy. Earlier subjects which we discussed will come to life as you gain knowledge in terminology, understanding concepts, and how they intermingle to deliver interested inquiries to you with each marketing campaign you launch. You'll learn tools to make your life easier and what tactics will work better than others in order to give you the advantage over your competition and to get the attention of your potential clients, solve their problems with special offers, and keep them for life with incentive building advantages and attention.

The best way to launch a successful marketing strategy begins with knowing your own business personality and goals, as well as knowing who your target potential customers are. The only difference between a profitable brand and an unprofitable brand is cohesiveness, keeping your company image in place throughout your business campaign; identity and recognition are the key elements.

In the next chapter you will begin taking action steps and assembling your rock-solid game plan.

CHAPTER FOUR

Building Your CDL Brand Step One - Know Yourself, Know Your Audience

By beginning the process with solid plans and goals, you will become a successful company and attain profits and growth much faster. You will be clear on your views of how to better your company as well as have the ability to see what isn't working currently.

Now that you have decided on what your ideal business strategy will be, it's time to begin putting your ideas on paper and hold yourself accountable to your ideas and plans.

What kind of business will you be?

A sole proprietorship?

A partnership?

A Limited Liability Company (LLC)?

A corporation?

Having a clear understanding of what each of these offers, the benefits and weaknesses of each, and where you feel you'll fit in the best, is an important decision and should be made with as much knowledge and clarity as is possible to have. A brief discussion of each follows.

If, however, after reading this you feel you don't have all the answers, do more reading. Talk to other operators or owners who run their business the way you would like to. Ask why they chose the path they did, then evaluate your options. It is always a good idea to speak with legal counsel also to make sure you are interpreting state regulations, federal mandates, and business structures in the correct manner. Misinterpretation can cost you your business—and your home and assets—down the road if made incorrectly in the beginning!

Sole Proprietorships

In this business profile, it is up to you and you alone. The Internal Revenue Service (IRS) sees a sole proprietorship as a default type of company, and will automatically label your business as such if it's not stated otherwise in legal documents and licenses, such as registering in your state as a business.

As a sole proprietorship, it is easier to keep costs low, as you have the control of spending and costs, which also simplifies record keeping. If you plan on building your company with multiple trucks and drivers. However, the greater possibility of accidents increases, as well as your liability, and therefore this can affect your personal assets substantially.

An Important Note - If you don't separate out your personal assets from your business assets, they are all seen as the same thing by the state and legal system. If, for example, you default on a loan or lose your truck without replacement from insurance, your home could be repossessed to repay financial debt or loans. If you have other truckers driving for you, this liability increases also, exposing you to higher possibilities of damage and recourse.

For these reasons, maybe being a sole proprietorship as a trucker isn't the best choice for a business structure. The risks for accidents and misuse is high for trucking companies, and these risks are—most of the time—out of your control.

Independent Contractors (vs. Employees in the Trucking Industry)

Many truck drivers fall into this category. They have their own truck, but work for another person to provide a service. They are not employees of the company, however, and govern their own income tax reporting and maintenance of equipment on their own. They are not hired as part of a company fleet, but can drive for companies who have them.

Because the person or company the independent contractor is working for doesn't take income tax out of their paycheck, they receive a 1099 form for income tax reporting purposes, and can also claim expenses and other costs as part of their 'business,' such as declaring loss of value in equipment and trucks. It is a good idea to anticipate the tax requirements and make quarterly estimated payments toward the annual income tax.

An independent contractor can operate as a partnership, LLC, or corporation, though this practice isn't common.

An employee of a trucking company receives a W2 and would have tax money taken out of each paycheck to cover income tax requirements.

Partnerships

Within the structure of a partnership, both parties share ownership of the business. Both have invested in the business and both are involved in its structure and operations. From this point forward, however, duties and responsibilities can be divided separately or combined.

Value for this business structure comes from the security of having shared responsibilities, which can give the company a sizable advantage when starting up. More resources are available, and more talent can be offered, as well as money.

But the losses also are shared, and as a partnership, both parties involved are still liable for any accidents, errors, losses, and damages. You and your partner are not separate from the business and if unforeseen events cause outside parties to file lawsuits against the business, both of you will be named. And if your company can't weather the damage, your assets may be vulnerable, including homes, financial accounts, and any other material items of value.

Even if you aren't the only person who may be held responsible for unfortunate occurrences, the risks are still evident and you won't be protected if something drastic happens.

The most common types of partners are:

General Partnerships - Both entities manage the business and are involved in the direct operations of the partnership. This includes responsibility of running the company, and sharing the liability as well as its profits and debts.

Limited Partnerships - This type of business relationship has an investor, one who fronts money to the company and in return profits from the growth and revenue the business produces. They also are considered liable for debts and losses the business may experience, but have little—if any—involvement in the running and operations of the company.

Corporations

Operating your business as a corporation has some notable advantages, and separation of your personal assets from the business is one of them. *If your business fails and debts must be accounted for, you won't lose your home to pay for them.*

Based on your profits and revenue, a corporation's tax responsibility can be high or low. They can also incorporate shareholders who contribute to the company initially, and are awarded dividends as compensation when the company is profitable. Investors can also contribute to a company's well-being, while expecting growth to come back to them if they decide to sell their 'portion' of the company, or if the company is sold down the road.

Several events must happen when a corporation is established.

- They must have annual meetings to discuss and report financial statuses, with official records of who attended the meetings and what was said. These are recorded as 'minutes' and also state situations at hand and who will be involved in the handling of them and must be kept on file for the corporation.

- An organization chart must be available for public notice, showing employee titles, the upward chain of command, and basic structure of management.

- Accounting and financial statements must be documented and approved by all managing personnel and shareholders.

- Legal documents must be assembled and filed for the company.

Beyond being a 'corporation,' there are still further organizational decisions to be made. Four options of corporations are available, and they are:

C-Corporations - This structure separates the profits and are taxed separately from the owners.

S-Corporations - Most often, these corporations are not responsible for income taxes. The profits and losses are passed through the company to shareholders who report them on their own individual tax returns.

Professional Corporations - These businesses are most often assembled under a common profession or common fields of interest. Liability rests with the owners for many losses brought about by the actions of the company.

Non-Profit Corporations - These organizations are tax-exempt and function for the sole benefit of their objectives. Most often, they are businesses functioning within fields of education, charity, communities, and philanthropy.

Due to the fact that corporations are more expensive and demand more organization than the other business profiles, independent truckers and contractors don't usually set up their businesses in this manner, though if they knew the consequences of certain situations, many would investigate the possibility of doing so.

Because the shareholders carry the brunt of the burden, trucking companies need to take a second look at organizing their companies as corporations. This provides protection for the company if a lawsuit were filed and put the business' future at risk. If only for this reason alone, it may be a wise decision to opt for a corporate structure of your trucking business.

Limited Liability Company (LLC)

This structure offers a little bit of each of the sole proprietorship, partnership, and corporation. The owners—or 'members,' as they are referred to—file taxes similarly as sole proprietorships and partnerships do. They list profits and losses on their personal tax filings. An LLC can also tax themselves as a corporation, if doing so would be prudent to the business' best interest. A single member can become an LLC if they see fit. Restructuring a sole proprietorship or partnership to an LLC can also be easily done, and often is when owners become aware of the advantages.

The options available for LLCs over the rigid requirements are preferred by many CDL operators; there are no meetings to conduct, no shareholders to answer to, and no lengthy legal document filings that need to be performed.

Yet, an LLC *provides you with the protection from personal losses and damage the company may incur.* The company may take the hit for any accidents or liability of drivers and have to reorganize or file for bankruptcy, but homes can't be lost and personal accounts can't be drained due to mishaps and damage.

Considering the new advances in transportation and vehicle self-drivers, the transport industry is most likely up for some changes in the future. When you consider all the trucks on the road and all the freight which needs to be moved, there will always be a place for drivers, yet industry moves on and changes are inevitable for our industry.

The description may change a bit and the way we 'drive' vehicles on the road could alter, but all in all, the trucking industry is still a safe and prosperous business to be involved in. Technology will offer us all some incredible discoveries and choices in the coming decades. Your choice to be a part of this ever-changing and growing industry is a wise one, provided you take precautions and make knowledgeable decisions.

As for choosing an option for the type of business you are going to start, you may want to ask yourself this:

> *'If I were to have a damaging event happen, perhaps one of my drivers being involved in an accident due to negligent driving (either eating or texting while driving), and I was sued for more money than the sum total of all my trucks,*

equipment, and business assets, would I want to risk losing
my property and personal assets to cover the suit?'

Answering this question may prove to be different between owners, depending on what state you operate out of and what your particular situation is. The structure should be to your company's benefit for success and for loss, and judging the factors is up to you as the business owner. Weigh your options, discuss options with professionals and family members, and set it up in the best way possible.

However, the future plays out, either entrusting your investments to drivers or depending on robotic technology to carry you through, striving for a profitable and growing business is what every owner/operator hopes for. Guarantee your success by studying the options and making the business decisions for you and your company.

Developing a Business Plan and Executive Summary

Your Mission Statement

By committing to a Mission Statement, you will have a reference for your own intentions and future business decisions. It will simplify your idea and brand, while giving you the roots of what you want your business to be and develop into. It doesn't have to be long and it can change as your business grows. We've mention and explain more about how to write your life's purpose and your mission and vision statement for your business in the book CDL Minded Entrepreneur, but for now, while you are beginning down the road to building your successful company, give yourself some foundational reference and compose a meaningful and sustainable mission statement.

- Keep it simple; one to two sentences is best

- Aim for under 20 words, 15 is better

- No fluff or fancy wording, be direct and precise

SAMPLE: *XYZ Company is committed to delivering products safely and efficiently across the Western Region of America.*

It's a good idea to keep your Mission Statement in sight, maybe as a sign on your desk or a sticker in your cab. Look at it often, and think about how you are accomplishing it day by day. Giving yourself a sense of accomplishment and pride is important, especially if you are a sole proprietor. You need to acknowledge your integrity and what you're doing it for as much as possible; no one else will be your cheerleader! And as you grow, you can also see how far you've come. Ideas are simple in the beginning, but as you succeed and grow and the complications of running your business become complicated, you'll value the simplicity of your mission statement and appreciate its directness and honesty.

What will be your service definition and what will you provide?

By examining a sample company, it's easy to see how your own will be similar as well as how you want to make it different.

> *Company XYZ sees an opportunity to offer better transportation options intrastate to farmers in the Midwest. Due to rural locations, rising fuel costs, and unreliable delivery dates, and LTL (less than truckload) shipments, XYZ believes it will be able to offer scheduled, combined pick-ups from regional areas of smaller farmers, developing a 'co-op' of delivery clients, and deliver the specific crops to nearby farmers markets and local stores for more reliable deliveries. By combining farmers' pick-ups and deliveries, XYZ will also be able to cut down on unnecessary trips, offering better prices to the farmers. The more the business plan sees success, the more areas XYZ will be able to offer their services too and build a reliable and cost-effective business. Farmers will also be offered incentives when they 'bring on' other farmers to join the delivery service. XYZ will focus on farm produce and products initially, but wants to eventually offer delivery services for grain, large crop harvests (such as corn and alfalfa), and perhaps dairy (consider growth and a 5 and 10-year plan).*

Have you thought of any additions you want to add to your business plan?

Do you have any ideas you are giving second thoughts to, perhaps thinking it may be too much work, too hard to find customers, or worry you're offering services to clients who may not even exist?

Examine a few companies you admire. Take note of their customer approach, comparing their image and marketing message as well as their size, growth, and what it must have taken to get them there.

By examining model companies and businesses, you will get a good idea of what you want to do and how you want to do it, as well as the negative things you definitely don't want to do in your business!

Put pen to paper.

Begin to write down your decisions now, and compare some aspects as you examine who you want to be as a business, who you believe your customers will be, how you think you will succeed in your industry, and what it will take to get your goals achieved.

Start with three columns, titled:

Current Views   **Possible Changes**   **New Ideas**

Answer the following questions in your chart. Keep it brief, but thorough. If you find you need more columns, add a 'Notes' column for each question to think about after you've completed this section.

What specific needs will your company require?

- Specific freight equipment needed, particularly for different types of freight

- Truckload (TL) or less than truckload (LTL) hauling

- Interstate or intrastate hauling

- Long haul, over the road, or specific geographic regions

Are you a one-person show, or will you have a team?

- Will you be the only driver with one truck, and have an owner/operator company?

- Will you be hiring other drivers, immediately or soon after you build revenue?

- What will be needed in addition to drivers?

- Back-office support

- Dispatch services

Before you open for business, what will you need?

If your company will be running its own truck(s), you will either need to purchase your fleet or have them financed. You'll need to find an equipment financing company to support your needs as well as insurance, an electronic logging device (ELD, required for insurance coverage), and drug and alcohol testing provider (also required for insurance). You will need to be compliant with the Federal Motor Carrier Safety Administration (FMCSA), and could possibly need help in seeing how to become compliant. In addition, you may want to use a *factoring company* or *fuel card provider*, making it easier to keep your fleet ready and available.

By doing a bit of research on these items and gathering opinions and reviews on specific price quotes and experiences, you will gain the knowledge you need in order to customize and move forward with your business plan, making sure you covered all the needed criteria and necessary logistics. If you are going to be traveling interstate, you will also want to research tolls and highway costs for interstate travel.

How will your company and its services differ from your competition?

Now that you've had time to think about your own business and how it will fit into the transportation industry you have chosen, it's time to drill down and be specific about your services.

- You've picked your region(s) for coverage

- You've chosen what types of hauling you'll focus on, and for what industries

- You've also decided on specialties which will differ you from other competition

If you haven't answered these specifics directly and know exactly how you are going to proceed with your business, then it's time to do this.

This is the 'fun' part of your business, because this is where you are the boss (which is why you began this in the first place), you choose the direction of your company (whether it will be you alone for the first few months until you get some revenue built up, or whether you will be leading a team of members and employees), and you will govern who your ideal customer is, their business, how you'll provide the best services to them, and how you will keep them loyal to you and come back to you for transportation needs time and time again.

While some of this may seem daunting and repetitive, being absolutely sure of what your company is providing and who you will be providing those services to is imperative; without these two pieces in place, all your other decisions will be 'what ifs' and you won't be able to build any kind of business on speculation and indecisiveness.

What will make your company stand out from your competitors?

What will be your unique value which sets you apart from your competition? Do you have a clean record and operate safely? Are your customers extremely satisfied with your service, and can you get testimonials from them saying so?

Building a great reputation as well as specifying your particular advantage over using another company will set you apart and draw in customers easier, while also satisfying your customers' needs to keep them engaged and satisfied.

What does your industry sector look like?

Is it growing?

Is it one which has 'seasons' of activity?

Are their locations you will focus on for heavy transportation?

Will you be focusing on full-loads or partial load transport?

By asking yourself these questions about your specific industry, you will be able to get a better picture of where you can find clients, and perhaps be able to identify a few additional customers in related niches who may benefit from using your services. You may also be able to see, with just a few changes here or there, other areas which can give you avenues for new business when times may slow down, or when seasonal changes occur.

But *thinking* you know your industry and actually digging in to find the numbers and facts to back up your opinions are the first steps to knowing how your niche behaves within your industry, its reaction to disruptions and change, and where your business will be placed within its growth patterns.

Also, see where your region is growing by researching some state revenue figures and where your sector's agriculture, industry, technologies, and entertainment areas are growing or reducing. In today's markets, don't assume anything is the same as it was 6 months ago.

As a drastic example, farmers who provided produce to solely restaurants and civic centers have been left without any customers to sell their perishables to. They are looking to almost give their products away, to not only keep their own business and workers moving forward, but in hopes the pandemic will subside and business will once again give them the level of sales they are accustomed to.

By providing a means to get their goods to other parts or customers, you may be able to solve their problem and provide viable resources for yourself, all in one contract. By brainstorming with potential clients, you may be able to produce an entire branch of delivery for your company you had no idea existed, and neither did your client!

Where are your potential customers?

Do you have preexisting customers who will use your services when you 'open' your business, or will you be starting without a client base? Having relationships with brokers and shippers may benefit your business while you build your company and services. Load boards may also be a good way to keep your truck(s) moving and money coming in while you are building your client base. There are many available; some cost a membership fee and others are free. If you offer services interstate, these may be of particular help. Remember, use them as little as possible, they are expensive and cost you revenue.

By creating and maintaining good relationships with the connections that provided you customers, you can not only provide long term connections but you can have the opportunity to create everlasting relationships with the shippers. And if the relationship goes sour between the broker and the shipper, or some other factor plays into their absence, you will have an established and reliable customer without having to regain trust. DO NOT, however, lure customers away from a broker or dispatch shipper; doing so will tarnish your reputation and leave you without clients or shipments very quickly. News travels incredibly fast when there is a rotten apple in the bushel.

What do you know about your competitors?

Is your business so specific that you won't have any competition and you have to convince your customers they need your services, or will you be among a few or many in your transportation service?

Take some time to get acquainted with the other companies who do business in your region, with your potential clients, and the transportation itself when comparing successful long-term companies, how many are in business, and where their biggest clients are coming from.

By doing some analysis on your competition, you will discover areas which they aren't providing necessary service. If they are delivering incredible numbers of hauls out-of-state, yet missing the needs of an intrastate niche, make note of that and see if you can fill the need. Just because they are bigger or have been in the business longer, that doesn't mean they will be the do-all service for their clients.

How do you picture growth and goal achievement?

Why do you want to start your own CDL trucking business? Why do you want to be your own boss? Focus on the reasons which have brought you to this place and keep them in your plans as you grow. There is no better incentive than to see your dreams become realities, and making sure you see those dreams come to life will feed more dreams and more realities, building your business and solidifying success.

What is your short-term growth plan?

The break-even point – when your revenue coming in and the expenditures going out are equal.

There is no loss, but there is no gain. By knowing what your 'break-even point' is, you will be able to better judge your costs and what you'll need to charge to keep your company running. Some businesses achieve this within the first year, others can take some time to achieve it.

You'll need to factor in your trucks' payments (if they are financed), fuel costs, etc., and move toward the 'break-even point' as quickly as possible, while still being competitive and marketable in your niche. Maintaining a steady and reliable cash flow is a necessary first step to achieving this. Then you'll determine what you need in order to support yourself as an 'employee' and add it into your short-term plan. Don't forget payroll in the equation, namely yours.

What is your long-term growth plan?

If you are beginning as a sole-proprietor and being the only driver in your company, but later want to grow and add more drivers and trucks, you will need to consider the additional costs and upkeep of adding more trucks, hiring drivers, and developing supporting finance expenses (dispatch, payroll, office maintenance).

A portion of all your profits should be going back into the company to keep cash flow steady, but if you are hoping to expand, you should also be contributing a portion of your revenue to an account which will act as a 'buffer' if you fall onto hard times or want to expand your business in the future. This fund will also become a viable means of safety for your company if you fall on a 'drought' of clients or need to cover an unexpected expense with the truck(s), cargo claim disputes, or covering ill personnel.

Financial Planning and Profits

Making a profit and what it takes to do it isn't simple and it isn't easy, but if you understand some basic principles and start with all your records and finances in one centralized place, it will only be a matter of entering figures and depositing checks.

What does it take to make a profit?

Here's the formula: Revenue minus Expenses equals Profit

R - E = Profit

If you predict your expenses and revenue in a systematic way, you will be able to see where your business starts, how it progresses, where growth or decline occurs, and how it happens. You will also be able to see what determinations have to happen in order for you to achieve your small-growth plan, and eventually, your long-term goals.

Income Statement Projections

This financial sheet will be a *projected or estimated* summary of your complete plan. It is made up of four integral parts. You may also need these projections if you intend on applying for financial business loans, intend to have investors, or want to apply for federal funding or grants.

Expenses - the costs it will take to run your business

Revenue - income you will receive from your customers for your services

Net Income - the amount of money which remains from your Revenue once you have deducted the Expenses

Income Statement - the summary of these figures and projections; your financial tool which lists the Revenue, Expenses, and any other particulars during a specific period of time (it can also be referred to as a Profit and Loss Statement, or P & L Statement)

To figure out your projected expenses and profits, you will either need to rely on your own past experiences (if you have driven your truck before) or do some research. You can talk to other trucking companies as a potential client and get rates. You can research your expenses, as we've talked about earlier. And you can use any other method to get answers you may be able to think of, such as speaking with others who own their own companies (you may want to make sure they are not in the niche you are going to do business in). Asking for advice is always a great way to get information.

While you are doing your research, you will come across two terms which may not be familiar to you

Variable Costs – These expenses are generally linked to the costs you will incur during a haul, such as fuel, food, maintenance, repairs, and lodging. The total of each will be different each time, even if the route is a reoccurring one. Variable costs will be a bit harder to determine, so when you are listing costs, error on the high side to begin with. It won't take long before you understand the different degrees of variance and can produce a figure closer to the actual costs.

Fixed Cost – The consistent costs of fixed amounts is much easier to determine, and rarely varies from one run to another. These include purchase payments (of your truck and/or office), insurance, and payroll if you have one. You will also divide your annual costs by 12 for a monthly figure for toll passes and license renewals, and add them to your monthly costs also.

You will also want to determine your *target rate-per-mile (RPM)*, which is an estimate of the revenue you need to earn per each mile driven. This will help you establish a baseline for figuring if a bid will bring your company a profit or a loss. *Estimate your desired monthly profits (begin with your break-even point and add 10% to 15%), then divide that number by the number of miles you will drive in a month.*

With these cost figures in place, you will be able to find your *break-even point.* This will tell you how much your trucking company needs to generate in revenue to cover all your expenses. Keep in mind, this is not what your company needs in order to be profitable; this is the bare minimum you need in order to not lose money. This amount will give you a base figure of what you will need to charge in order for your company to 'break even.' Keep in mind, this is a figure which does not include any money going to you personally, unless you have added a figure in for your own monthly payroll.

Here is an example of what your expenses may be and how to organize them; yours can be different, depending on your business profile.

Expenses (when applicable)	Costs
Origination and development	$
Insurance	$
IFTA	$
Equipment	$
Fuel	$
Monthly fees, passes, permits, subscriptions	$
Other	$

Of course, you may have more or less entries in your summary. By including all the possibilities here you will have, you will be able to put together a more decisive and precise estimate for your projections and strategy.

Your Executive Summary

By combining all the sections you've just worked on, you will now have the basis of your business's Executive Summary. This document will give you the entire picture of your new business. Its components include:

Company Description

- Company Name - the title your company will operate as

- Services Provided - state what you will be doing; *'truckload or less than truckload freight services'*

- Company Goals - list the main objective for operating your business; *'to grow from being a one operator company to having three drivers within the first year'*

- Mission Statement - drop in your Mission Statement here; *'Our business believes in putting the customer first, keeping their freight safe and secure'*

- Key Personnel and Their Job Descriptions - list you and your employees and the tasks they will be doing; *'Owner - me; Manager - Jesse Tatum; Contractors - Grant LaFey, Trevor Haines'*

- Differentiating Qualities of Services - list your redeeming qualities as a CDL operator for your customers; *'10 years of experience in providing efficient and reliable delivery, industry expertise, and affordable pricing'*

- Optionally, you can also include a vision statement, which talks about the future of your business - where you want to go, and what you're striving for

Company Strategy

- Industry Description - this includes what you'll be doing and where you'll be doing it; *'Intrastate transportation of agricultural goods within Mississippi'*

- Customer Description - this names your clients and customers; *'Farmers and growers found on load boards and produce directories'*

- Competitor Description - a brief description of who you'll be vying for customers with; *'small to midsize operators with similar knowledge of CDL operating'*

- Strategic Partners - people and businesses which will support you in your operations and growth; *'Fuel card companies, ABC Mechanics, Growers of the Northeast Delta'*

- Competitive Advantages - list the things you offer which your competition does not; *'24/7 pick-up, co-op team advantages, efficiency, and combined rate offers'*

- Applicable Regulation - a list of your regulating organization alliances; *'state transportation regulators, state business regulators, FMCSA'*

- Growth Plan - 1 to 5 years goal and growth goals: *'one driving operator, increasing to 2-3 trucks and operators within 6 months, Year 2 to offer dairy pick-up also, Year 5 to increase both lines to 5 trucks/operators*

Financial Estimates

Discuss how you will meet financial obligations and maintain positive cash flow. By detailing the process below, you will cover all angles of your financial strategy.

- Variable Expenses: Direct - fuel

- Variable Expenses: Indirect - factoring, lodging, meals

- Total Variable Expenses: add both columns for totals

- Fixed Expenses: Direct - insurance, passes, subscriptions

- Fixed Expenses: Indirect - office rental/payments, business permits, payroll

- Total Fixed Expenses: add both columns for your totals

- Break Even Revenue Calculation: the formula follows, don't be intimidated, just take the figures from the columns above, and you'll have this figure

- Revenue - Variable Costs = the Contribution Margin

- Contribution Margin ÷ the Total Revenue = Contribution Margin Ratio

- Fixed Costs ÷ the Contribution Margin Ratio = Break-Even Revenue

As you can see, many factors determine your financial estimates, and knowing as much as you possibly can about this part of your business can only be beneficial. You can also hire an accountant to analyze your Executive Summary and determine ways you can cut costs, increase revenue, invest in products or systems which will serve your business, and guide you with needs for tax filing and payroll strategies (insurance, PTO, W2, etc.). But if you've kept up with what we've discussed here, you have constructed a firm business profile and established criteria necessary for opening up your business.

BUSINESS PLAN
Linear Icons

Marketing

Now that you have completed the Executive Summary, you are half-way to outlining your marketing strategy. You only have to decide on what marketing path you want to take and begin the process.

Here are the accomplishments you've made so far. You've done some hard work deciding the particulars of your business. Now for the fun stuff!

1. You have a very good idea of who your potential customers are.

2. You've done research and know where you can find your potential customers, or at least where to start.

3. You know who your competitors are, directly and indirectly.

4. You know the strengths and weaknesses of your industry and how your company fits into the industry niche.

5. You know what your own strengths are.

6. You know the profile of your own company and how you want the industry to see you.

7. You have a good idea of how your finances stand, where your money is, and how much you have to work with to promote your business.

Nailed it!

Now all you have to do is learn a few ins and outs of marketing, decide how you want to begin your strategy, and lay the groundwork for the marketing to build from.

Defining Your Target Audience

Being aware of your own direction gives you the outline of who you are looking for as potential customers and clients. If you are focused on hauling milk, you look for dairies. Simple, right?

Yes and no.

Yes, the dairies are a great place to start, but who else could benefit from your services? By expanding your boundaries and thinking outside the box, you will not only increase your client base and target audience, but you will have an upper hand on your competition.

Though milk transport is very specific, let's use another example to explore these ideas and get the creative juices flowing.

We've used the farmers' extra produce example before, let's try and see if we can stir any other possibilities for business while hauling produce.

Line up the necessities you need to transport lettuce, tomatoes, bell peppers, and green beans to the farmers market. The produce will be in sturdy boxes, and you'll be using a refrigerated trailer. Chances are, if you are picking up produce from independent farmers, you will be making several stops in rural communities before the major route to the market.

Who will you pass on the way?

Are there dairies who may have cheese or specialty products they would want to sell at the market too? What about the baker around the corner who bakes bread in exchange for eggs at the dairy? Or the lady with a new flock of hens who are producing enough eggs to feed an army? And maybe the melon farmer has too many to sell at his roadside stop; would he want to have his excess melons transported too?

How do you find out about these businesses, though?

You can look up the dairy, sure enough. And perhaps you'd see the melon farmer on the side of the road. But what about the baker? Or the lady with too many eggs? How do you find out about them?

You dig into your niche by way of *engagement*. And this is where your knowledge in social media, conversation, and upbeat involvement can make you a personality in your niche and bring you success instead of an Out of Business sign.

Remember, a strong identity of what your business offers gives you clarity in determining how to set up your business structure. By creating a Business Plan and Executive Summary, you give your business a road map of who you are, what you offer, and where you want to go.

In Step 2, we'll delve into the specifics of assembling your brand image and strategy, as well as approaching the task from your customers' point of view.

CHAPTER FIVE

Building Your CDL Brand Step Two - Incentives, Referrals, and Loyalty Programs

Before you begin to design your marketing program and take time to learn its concepts and tools, you need to understand why targeting is so important to your success. You have the basics, but there are just a few more tips which will change your game plan from good to great.

If you already have one or two great customers, focus on their needs and see how you solve them. Why do they come to you for services? Why are you their preferred choice over the company which is actually closer to their business? By answering a few questions, you can come up with key elements you'll want to exploit in your marketing campaigns and strategy.

Furthermore, wasted time is wasted effort, and it costs you money in the long run. By not being clear on who you are the best transportation service for, you will lose clients simply because they've come up with their own conclusion of what you offer. By trying to cover too many services or gather customers in an industry you are not familiar with, you will depict a lax dedication or be labeled as an imposter in the industry. You'll be doing more harm than good to your company, and the customers won't even look at your costs or details.

Honesty in business (transparency) is not only 'gold' for success, but it's the only policy towards success. Being transparent to your clients and customers is not taking credit for being the best in your sector, no matter how small, and will draw your ideal customers. These are the people who will not only call you every time without pricing out competition, but they will spread the word of how great your service is and how pleased they are to have found you. When a customer is this happy with you, they will go to the ends of the earth to celebrate your success. They are your 'champions' and can illuminate even the darkest of times.

We've talked about this many times already.

Having this business structure is exactly where you want to be as a beginning business owner in the CDL transportation business. There are other lines who will undercut your prices and there are other companies who will promise quicker delivery. But if you offer sincere integrity, great specialized service, and, above all, individualized customer care, you will bring back those customers time and time again, and they will lay your path to business success.

Now, you will find out how doing all this over-the-top customer care will come back to you in profits!

What price will you pay to find your customers?

In other words, how far will you go to uncover the secret location of your perfect clients?

Will it be the expense of time it takes you to learn how to launch a business website?

Will you spend considerable time designing your website so you can attract your ideal customer?

Will it be the money you paid for the list of potential businesses in the region that you are covering?

Or will it be thousands of dollars you expect to pay for the advertising ads you intend to post?

When you think about getting more customers and how you might go about finding them, who do you think will know the personalities of your potentials, aside from you?

Who has the knowledge of how your business performs, directly?

Who knows the care you take in loading freight, the extent you'll go to when you promise you'll deliver 'on time,' or the extra precautions insured to run a mechanically sound and maintained truck and trailer?

Who has, without a doubt, the best description of how you saved their full load shipment of fresh frozen flounder from thawing in the Arizona sun when a well-known shipping company (who won't be named) used a 30- year old refrigeration trailer, pulled from decommission, to deliver your 'high-end shipment' to a 5-star restaurant?

Exactly, *your present customers.*

Number 1 - Your Current Customers and the Cost of Customer Acquisition

The people who call you, no matter the freight, no matter the destination, because they know you will do whatever it takes to take care of their needs. And you'll do it with a smile, with a fair rate, and best of all, with their best interests at heart.

These companies, these people, your customers, are your best promoters, and usually, they are the least expensive too. Since you have shown them exactly what you do in order to deliver the best service possible, they will sing your praises and do whatever it takes to make sure you are known as the 'best in your business,' especially if you respond to their individual needs and have an engaged client relations program.

Remember, your clients are smart too, they are loyal, and their best interests are in your success. Without you being in business and surviving, they will be left in the cold without the attention and care you've shown consistently. They deserve to be shown appreciation and attention.

For you, they are also your best marketing tool.

So, with all this power of their word and praise, how can you turn their loyalty into new clients?

Show your gratitude with more than your voice

First and foremost, don't forget their loyalty. Before using their testimonials or referrals, make sure they realize how thankful you are for their words. You don't have to give them a discount on their next shipment in order for them to respect and recognize your gratitude. Although, this would be a highly appreciated service!

Build a referral program for them and use incentives to create a two-way street of growth and prosperity. This all begins with a conversation and being interested and engaged with your customers.

Making personal and unique contact with each customer is easy.

- Send a handwritten 'thank you' note after shipments, especially to new customers or for a particularly unique haul or circumstance. Receiving this in the mail will catch their attention also, and double the response and appreciation.

- You also have an easy tool at your fingertips by sending an email or post, saying thank you for their business, or commending them on a special success.

- Post a picture or a quick video on your website about an experience or how a customer made your day will also show a sense of appreciation and comradery.

These little 'gifts' stand out from the everyday experience and are treasures; your customers will remember your thoughtfulness for a very long time. These gestures will set you apart from your competition also, gaining devotion and loyalty with only a few keystrokes or stamps.

Referral programs offer something in return

How do you ask a customer for an endorsement without being pushy? It isn't as hard as it sounds and it can be done in a creative manner. By engaging your loyal customers, you are giving them the chance to become more involved with you, if they choose, and also be rewarded for their efforts with something you choose to offer. Here are some ideas to get you started.

- Offer two free tickets to the movies for posting a short comment of their recent experience with you to your Facebook page.

- Have a contest for a two-night get-away at the local bed & breakfast for the Best Karaoke Video, creating a song about your company and singing its praises.

- Combine rewards for your existing client as well as the clients they 'bring in.' The reward doesn't need to be related or expensive, but it should be considered a reward for both clients.

Here are a few 'tips' which will make your program more successful and produce happier customers.

- Be very clear, upbeat, and honest when promoting your program. Post the terms clearly and make sure there is a place for questions if they have any. State the contest in a positive manner and don't make it sound as if you are 'fishing' for compliments or recognition. Your program has a very large chance of backfiring if this happens, so have someone else read it over and make sure it is only asking for honesty in a very gracious way.

- Make it easy to sign up for. Make needed links obvious and post conditions and terms prominently. Post the contest or program on all your marketing media. Once again, making sure you are clear about the participation and terms they may have to abide by. Signing up should also be easy to understand and simple to do.

Ask for their thoughts with surveys

You can also send out customer surveys asking about their experience after a shipment is delivered or how they like the new invoicing process. This gives your customers an easy way to give you feedback. You also can pull analysis results from them which, depending on how you ask them, can give you ranking within your industry, confidence in your ability to deliver on time, or ease of using your online scheduler. You can even find out how many of your clients rate you 'excellent' or find the percentages of returning customers who would use your services again. By posting at the beginning of the survey that all responses are anonymous, your answers will be more honest and give you information which otherwise might be hard to collect.

You can also add a block which is an 'open' response, allowing your customers an opportunity to give individual feedback. You may receive critical responses, yes, but don't overlook these gems; they are opportunities for you to make a situation right by stepping forward to correct a mistake or fix a problem. You may not turn everyone's opinion around, but more often than not, taking the initiative and doing your best to make things right will create respect and, possibly, an opportunity for a second try. In the very least, you will learn of discord in your business and can fix the problem.

Take their words to the bank - referrals & testimonials

If you find yourself able to use direct quotes from your customers, use them. Be very careful that you quote their response *exactly* as they state it. Don't feel you need to build it up or correct their grammar. The beauty of quotes is the tone in which they are said, and unique nuances and intellect shows the individual personality, diversity, and sincerity of your patrons.

Use them creatively also, and always make sure you have their permission. Even if they have given their permission before, ask again if you want to re-use a comment or draw on a new one. Never assume anything when you are stating a person's comments and signing their name to it publicly.

Try these, or create your own ways of promoting, the options are endless:

- On the side of your truck, you could put a sideline under your business name, in a small cursive script, (on a removable magnetic sheet would be best); *'Best Truck Service This Side of the Mississippi' - Dalton Dairy.*

- Or you can add a quote under the subtitle on your website; *'Delivered My Goods When No One Else Would' - Beverly Handly.*

- And don't forget the brief video of George's elated smile when you pulled in with his chickens which had been 'lost' in Wichita, but your truck saw the broken down trailer and brought the cluckers 'home;' *'They helped the original broken-down truck move my chicken crates to their empty truck and finished the route- I didn't lose a single bird!' - George Hastings, Hastings Flock & Fowl.*

The more you use your referrals and testimonials, the more you will realize new opportunities where their support can be used to spread your message. Satisfied customers are like nuggets of gold; you must protect them and do everything you possibly can to keep them in your possession. It isn't an impossible task; by being honest, grateful, attentive, and sincere, you will collect priceless marketing advantages over any competitors 'deal' or 'promotion.'

Number 2 - A Website

While it seems unimaginable for you to launch a website, it can be done fairly easily, and you can do it by yourself if you do a bit of reading, have a laptop or computer, and a connection to the internet.

You will need to purchase a web host. They are the techies who play the part of gatekeeper to your website, they are in charge of keeping your website 'up' and available, they support the site when things go wrong, and they can provide extra services such as email and security walls for you, and quite often offer many other services (you may never use). According to Brad Smith, Editorial Staff at Hosting Facts.com, the Ten Best Website hosting services are, based on speed, uptime, and costs are (as of February 2020):

1. Bluehost - Best Overall

2. HostGator Cloud - Best Cheap Cloud (has a lot of information storage)

3. Hostinger - Cheapest Price

4. GreenGeeks - Best 'Green' Hosting

5. DreamHost - Pay Monthly, No Higher Renewals

6. SiteGround - Best Customer Support

7. A2 Hosting - Fastest Shared Hosting

8. WestHost - Great Uptime for the Price

9. GoDaddy Hosting - Reliable, Good Extra Features

10. Site5 - Unmetered Storage

While each has a benefit listed, don't totally rely on this to make a choice. Go to this link for the full review of each (yes, do it!) and a chart of 30 of the most popular host services and their ranking highlights.

Best Web Hosting (2020) Hosting Facts

Depending on which host you choose, you may have website design services included with the cost, or you can use free services, such as WordPress, SquareSpace or Wix. Or, click here for a recent article of the latest and greatest according to Website Builder Expert: 11 Best Free Website Builders.

Take the time to read through these sites and articles. When you finish (might take you 20 to 30 minutes, a bit longer if you want to become an expert), you'll know all about website design and building, web hosting, and how to pick the one which will be the best for your business. If you still haven't found an exact fit, do some research and read a few independent articles (not the ones which are paid-for ad listings at the top of the search pages). There, you will find the best information.

Number 3 - Become Part of the Social Media Connection

Being savvy with social media isn't just a 'trend' that's set aside for the techies and the younger generations. These days, everyone is connected to the Internet, especially since lock-downs and social distancing have become a mandate due to the pandemic. If your business isn't present online, you are failing at keeping connected, and being connected is the bloodline of your trucking operation.

In a recent survey of CDL operators, when asked what social media platform truckers prefer (TruckersNews, D. Hollis Feb. 2020), Facebook led the pack at 63% surveyed. YouTube followed at 54%, 15% preferred Instagram, and 14% liked LinkedIn the best. Surprisingly,

Twitter came in around 13%, followed by Pinterest at 11%. Here's the full article Truckers Favor Facebook, Which Turns 15 Today [2]. Can you figure out another reason why this article may be important for a business?

If you were running an ad on a social media platform for truckers, where would you get the most viewing? Yes, Facebook, according to this article. But since your target audience isn't truckers (well, probably not), then this won't be any more of a passing interest note and connection to a like-minded individual such as yourself.

But, after reading the article, you can see the power of social media, especially for you and your CDL business. If your targeted client is also consumed by their business and unavailable most of the day, unable to view your ads on social media, when they do eventually connect with these social sites it can be incredibly powerful, especially if they were thinking earlier in the day they should try a new transportation line for their products. Customers looking for quick solutions to their problems are in every crack and crevice of your niche. Never underestimate the power of social media. As you become more familiar with the 'producing' side of social media, you will understand how important having your business present online and how simple and cost-effective the resources can be.

By having an online presence, you are also providing your intended customers and clients a resourceful place to get more information than what a television ad or radio spot can offer. It spotlights your specialties, gives an in-depth account of your business philosophy, acknowledges the specifics of your particular niche, and offers personal interest articles and access if they want to get questions answered, even when they are viewing your site at 11 at night.

When you see all the benefits that having a current and interactive website offers your potential as well as established customers, you can also see how it will be the command center of your marketing campaigns, at affordable prices with a reach of thousands.

Tying your online presence with traditional advertising

There are a million and one ways which are advantageous to running a multi-level campaign for your business. That is, if you have a million and one dollars to spend, and if you have the time to sketch out and purchase all the supporting space, time, and schedules which are needed to launch such an elaborate crusade.

The simple fact is that, with a few clear ideas and a couple of sensible actions, your marketing launch stating you're *open for business* doesn't have to take any longer than a few hours, some creative ideas, and a collective plan (and maybe just a few dollars to get the ball rolling).

When you have your website up and running, you can create emails, send newsletters, create blog posts, and begin discussions on industry trends. The more clients, customers, and interests you add to your email list, the more opportunity you have to create a business and bring in added revenue. There are many tools by which you can gather email addresses for promotions and print flyers to get your name recognized.

But first, you need an image, something which will be recognizable to your customers immediately and can resonate in your industry with your business attached. You need a logo.

Design something simple, clean, usable, and recognizable. Think car vectors; they are logos, such as the Mercedes-Benz circle or the Subaru oval with the constellation. They all symbolize something specific within the company, yet are simple, identifiable, and recognizable to the outside world.

Try to not get too wrapped up in this process. But also pick something which you can live with, as you will be using this on everything, as an icon by your business name, next to your website address in the search bar, on the invoices you bill out, as well as the newsletters you connect to your audience with. It will be emblazoned on the doors of your truck and possibly on the sides of your trailer(s). Think of this logo as the 'face' of your business, with the design depicting your business' personality and image.

If you need a designer to help you come up with a few ideas, check out Freelancer or Upwork. They will be able to give you some different samples and you won't have to spend a fortune for the artwork. You can work out the terms for your contract, say maybe two edits or five designs. You know the secret though: simple and specific.

This design will be the foundation of all your marketing strategies and it will be recognizable within your industry and throughout your audience, if you use it wisely and market yourself in strategic places.

Always remember...

It's easier to keep customers happy, than trying to win them back. Make sure once you have a customer, you keep the connection fresh, relevant, interesting, and above all else, *all about them.*

When building your marketing strategy, use the same words, logos, and bylines; repetition is a good symptom of recognition.

In the next chapter you will learn easy tools to use for client engagement and retention within your focused and specific niche.

═══════
═══════
═══════
═══════
═══════
═══════
═══════
═══════

CHAPTER SIX

Building Your CDL Brand Step Three - Reach Your Clients and Grow Your Business

Use the Right Niche Channels to Grow Your Outreach

Your website is up, you have a logo in place to use throughout your marketing, and you've realized the strength of online and traditional media tools for your promotions. In this chapter, you will learn how to put these strategies into action and interactive methods of applying the best means needed to achieve your goals.

You've also seen by researching a few things here and there that you don't need a lot of money to promote your business to your niche. Knowing how to assemble your strategy using free, inexpensive, or incentive-driven services can give you the means to reach your target audience while still maintaining your budget. Being specific with your strategy will keep the promotion focused while promoting directly to your audience; identify the right channel for your promotion and you will connect with your customers in a meaningful way. Also, if this is your first website or business launch, learning for free is much better than learning at a high price.

Facts are facts; if you don't get your amazing service in front of the amazing customers who will benefit from your services, your business will go nowhere. You also know that, with the right strategy, you can send the perfect message that will resonate with your potential customers.

So which marketing methods and channels are right for you?

We've talked a lot about strategy, but how do you figure out what 'strategy' is best for your business? We'll go a bit deeper to get specific about the terms and clarify what would work best to reach your customers.

You already know what your perfect customer profile looks like. Whether it's the retail purchaser at the department store downtown or the medical supply coordinator at the hospital, you know who you can provide the best services to and why they will love your company.

You not only know where this customer lives but you know the websites they visit as well as the activities they do in their spare time. Or do you?

Do you know what websites your ideal customer visits? Do you know what activities interest them and where they might spend their time? You probably do, but chances are you may not realize it yet.

By putting together a strategy, you will get your message in front of your ideal customer without too much effort or money. If your ideal customer would have you ship racks and racks of clothes from NYC to Los Angeles, this person probably spends time on trending websites for clothing, maybe the most popular blog on similar items like shoes for women or affordable clothes for teens. Place an ad on like-minded sites for connection.

How do you find the sites your customers visit? Think like your customer and make a list of the keywords you think your customer would use to search for their interests.

'Latest fashions in Europe'

'Cheapest clothes for women'

'Comfortable and affordable pants for men'

'Dress displays and racks'

Whatever you think your customer might search, type it in and see where you go. You may hit a dead end, but you may also find a few niches which you hadn't thought of. Also, scroll down your search list and see what words are popular in the descriptions of the sites. Here, other tidbits of information can be found which may lead you down a profitable path...

If you type in a word in Google and then hover over the search bar, you'll get some related terms to the word you typed. There are also some sites that can give you keywords similar to your own words. Try WordStream to give you more options for keywords and phrases related to your searching. They offer free trials, but do charge for access after a certain amount of time.

Most likely, your ideal customer spends quite a bit of time online. Will your customer read the news, catch up on blogs, check email, online shop, or download games? See if you can find out where your competitors are advertising. If they are spending money, chances are they feel like they are in a successful place to spend more money to advertise. Check it out.

As you investigate the options, you will also, no doubt, come across apps which say they can save you time and money and assemble a marketing program, quick and easy for you. Some of these are great, others can be useless. Approach them with caution, and always make sure you know what they are talking about. If the site keeps on using phrases or terms you are unfamiliar with, find out what the phrases mean too, know exactly what they offer and how it works. Some sites can also be expensive and could promise you the world (such as 'you'll receive over 40,000 views in 24 hours'); be smart, be wise, and investigate with a wary eye.

To show several methods of marketing to a specific audience, let's examine a few examples.

Scenario 1

Interstate CDL business, ABC Freight, wants to increase their customer base for coast to coast dry freight. This company has 20 trucks, and uses independent drivers when needed. For the past 2 months, business has dwindled, grounding 2 to 4 trucks each week with no business for their independent drivers, who are now moving to other companies for business. ABC Freight needs more schedules, preferably from container docks, which are fast easy business for them. They choose to run several TV advertisements in New York/New Jersey, Savannah, and Virginia for the East Coast, Los Angeles, Long Beach, and Oakland on the West Coast, and Houston and Miami for the southern ports. They will support these spots with the same promotion in the TV ads, with promotional email notices to all their existing customers, offering 10% off scheduled deliveries for the next 2 weeks. They have designed landing pages to accept the clicks posted on their emails, as well as stated phone numbers and website addresses on the TV ads. The home page on their site also has the promotion positioned in their banner at the top of their site as well as an upper half-screen 'ad,' which will load prominently on any device, computer, laptop, phone, or tablet.

TV production costs – $2,500.00

TV schedule on regional demographic specific channels – $550,000.00

Design and post of home page and new landing page – $500.00

Email promotion (writing, design, link insert, and email address sort) - $450.00

Total Promotion Costs $553,450.00

New Customers - 15

Existing Customers Scheduled - 28

If ABC Freight wanted to see the value of their advertising investments by translating it into cost per new schedule, they could send out a survey after attaining the new clients to see where they had learned about the promotion. Or, they could have had a check-box on the scheduling page or when they spoke to your scheduler to set up their haul asking where they had learned about the promotion. This would be a very sensible idea and, with ABD Freight being a large company, chances are they will have a similar analysis tool in place to see just how strong each of their promotional tools paid out.

Scenario 2

Northwest regional freight company, Joe & Jane's Flying Fish Freight, is hoping to expand into a few more states with longer hauls, building their pick-up base as well as expanding their delivery region outside their present region of Washington state. They offer guaranteed delivery of shipments in under 10 hours and believe even by extending their delivery area, they will be able to maintain their objectives. They've added two new trucks to their fleet and are hoping to bring in new customers in adjoining states. Joe & Jane's Freight has decided to do all of their promotion online, using their own blog posting on their website (they have 500 followers) and also a direct email launch. They plan on featuring a three-email series of videos, focusing on company values, driver profiles, and specialty truck innovations which set them apart from other delivery companies in the state. Throughout the videos, they will portray their value, ingenuity, sincerity, and connections to existing customers, as well as their initial business objectives and how they've grown in the past 2 years. Not everyone who follows their blog posts and who is on their email list is a customer.

Production of promo home page and landing page for scheduling online - $45.00

Production and editing of 3 videos with Joe and Jane and others - $250.00

Merge of emails for a 3-day send, 700 addresses - $25.00

Miscellaneous costs - $100.00

New customers - 5

Expansion of new customers into Oregon, deliveries to Idaho and Oregon

This campaign for Joe & Jane was extremely profitable. They gained 5 new customers, adding to their client base, and by doing so will be expanding into new regions for deliveries. With the agricultural opportunities presented by Oregon and Idaho, they are hoping to get return customers also, and will launch another promotion to the growers in these regions to make their new commitments even more advantageous.

These scenarios are both fictitious, but you can see how a marketing promotion can play out in specific situations. By combining methods and tools with a bit of ingenuity and planning, your company can profit greatly. You do need to plan, and you do need to know the tools and methods you are using to take advantage of all the options which will benefit your promotion.

Following below is a list of specific channels which can help you organize the strategy of your marketing. Discovering the many uses of how they can benefit a campaign may even trigger thoughts of your own on how to use their technique and approach.

Referral Marketing - This strategy builds from the generosity and word of mouth from your existing clients and customers, and should be used with every business, as a promotional campaign or an ongoing program.

Content Marketing - Any traditional or online marketing which educates your potential customers using specific wording for increased traffic on your website, clicks on your links, and followers who engage in your marketing.

Newsletters - These are excellent vehicles for your potential and existing email list. You can keep your readers up-to-date on a new discount offer, discuss the latest ruling on permit increase costs, or have a contest. It can be informational, promotional, an opinion, or sharing stories from the road. Use a free service, such as Canva, to make them appealing and entertaining.

Search Engine Optimization (SEO) - By using keywords and phrases, search engines draw organic traffic (people who are looking for information on terms you've included in your marketing) and list you or your publications on the results. By using these terms in your blog, you can also draw traffic to articles and ideas you have on your website.

Podcasts - You will see these offered more and more, as they are easy to produce and cost very little. Most are written as an educational lesson with an option to purchase something at the end. If you are the writer type, you could put together a 10-step program to teach drivers how to pack for a long haul or review the top 5 best travel mugs available.

Public Relations - Refers to business activity used in traditional media outlets, such as public gatherings, conferences, and events. You may sponsor a booth at an arts festival or donate to a worthy cause for a listing in their news bulletin.

Speaking Engagements - Industry conferences, trade show demonstrations, community growth events, and town halls all can be an avenue for your business awareness and presence. Keep an eye on the city and community dates for social gatherings which may benefit from your knowledge and guidance, as well as you from theirs.

Online Advertising - Includes the purchase of PPC (pay-per-click) ads, social network display ads, banner purchasing on websites, and promotional videos on YouTube.

Traditional (Offline) Advertising - Printed publications (brochures, business cards), radio ads and info interviews, TV advertising, magazine ads, and trade show booth promotions.

Email Marketing - A direct and resourceful way to reach your existing and potential customers, usually have shown some kind of interest, unless you are using a purchased email list. Campaigns can be run as automated (sending a message when they click on a link) or targeted (using your own list, for example) promotions. A tried and true strategy.

Sales Playbooks - The creation of specific actions, usually used when a lead list is involved, to move a potential customer into a purchasing customer.

Online Events - Includes online webinars, demonstrations, workshops, and education using online software; range in costs varies.

Offline Events - These are person-to-person or crowd events, and use trade shows, seminars, demonstrations, workshops, showcases, and customer appreciation events for building customer relations.

Utility Marketing - Software tools which stimulate traffic, sharing between users, and brand awareness.

Influencer Marketing - A practice used when building relationships with people in pre-established communities and gatherings; think of clubs, influential memberships, and elite social circles.

Partner Marketing - Co-marketing activities with other like-minded businesses which are launched simultaneously with another company with similar interests.

Social Media Marketing - Building engagement between people and businesses on established social network platforms, such as Facebook, LinkedIn, Pinterest, etc.

Community Building - The process of accumulating people and communities who support the same cause and join together to build growth.

As you read through this list, I'm sure you were able to focus on the methods you thought may help you design a campaign, while others definitely were not going to be of any help or advantage. That is the beauty of having a large choice of options for a specific directive outcome. These have proven valuable to someone and some industry as some point in time. The longer we promote, the longer this list will become.

The point is this: you know your company, you know what types of promotions are appealing to you and which ones you will stay clear of. Use the ones you like, expand in a couple of areas if you are curious to see how they may perform for you, and then evaluate and choose the better ones for you. In a year or two, perhaps your business will take a turn and something else will look more advantageous. There is also the proverbial growth thing; new methods and channels appear all the time. Something which sets your company on fire may not even be conceptualized yet.

When analyzing your promotion after its finish, be sure to attribute the correct channel with the correct result. The fact that you now have more customers can be due to the fact that you emailed out the availability of a refrigerated truck for hauling, but it also may be because your new driver connected with a group of haulers who were overworked and in need of some help in hauling produce.

Don't be afraid to mix it up and try new things. When you do, though, make sure you are changing just one item in your promotion, so when you evaluate its results to previous promotions, you are able to see specific differences instead of trying to guess which one of the three changes was responsible for its result.

Setting Goals and Working Optional Objectives

You may from time to time come up with a goal you want to achieve, perhaps delivering interstate or offering more options of freight contents, but you aren't quite sure how to reach the people who would be involved in this new pursuit.

When you are familiar with different channels and methods of assembling a promotion or service launch, go back to the basics. Picture your ideal customers.

- What are their characteristics?

- Where will you find them?

- Plan a strategy of reaching them with whatever means you believe will be successful.

236

By going back to the basics and starting with a new plan, you are thinking clearly on the focus of a new customer. You are also broadening your options for opportunity instead of reconstructing an old method with means which worked for one set of criteria, but aren't necessarily good for your new set of criteria. And, best of all, you are building your own marketing prowess, using all options, some of which may be new tools, and stretching your creativity in new ways. This is not only good for you personally, keeping you sharp and energized, but it also will keep you one step ahead of your competition.

You are the innovator, action taker, and decision maker.

You are creating new methods.

You have the advantage of using new ideas over old.

Every so often, you may get stuck on an idea, or use the same promotion too many times, resulting in poor interaction and growth. These are signs of a stagnant marketing offer. Make notes, record results, and move on. When you find a method which doesn't meet your expectations, analyze the promotion and the tools you used and see where the broken link is.

You may want to fix the link by changing just one little component, which can be as simple as a color on the landing page or a word in the header of your email letter. Whatever it is, change it and try again.

But if you feel it may be an entire revamp of the promotion, don't waste your time in procrastination or analysis. Make the change and move forward. Nothing wastes time and money more than the repetition of pondering a broken method.

As you do your research, analyze the best strategies to reach your ideal customers, launch those promotions, and search the results for most activity and best sales. Take notes and imagine the results of a change or two.

What can you do differently next time which may reach more viewers?

What engagement seems to bring more viewers to your social media page? What engagement seems to bring more viewers to your podcast? What engagement seems to bring more viewers on your website?

Would relating the blog to the promotion bring in more views and more possible customers?

Would you change anything?

And when you're ready to do it all again, take a big breath and dive right in; lather, rinse, repeat.

Don't forget...

Take a plan, run the analysis, and then outline realistically where you want to be in 6 months, 1 year, 5 years, and even 10 years into the future. A measurable vision can lead to realizing your goals down the line; keep on reinventing your channels and methods, your strategies, and your promotions. When you're done, do it all again!

In the last chapter we'll be wrapping up your plan and taking it to the next level.

CHAPTER SEVEN

Your Successful Launch

tarting a business is more than just loading up your trailer and driving into the sunset. It is a work of love, and every effort brings you closer to achieving your dream of owning a successful and thriving business. You've also realized there are a few things you'll need to learn, and probably learn again. The best part about your venture is this:

You are the boss.

You govern the direction, and

You are able to plan your own future.

When you have run a few promotions, you'll be able to govern your channels better and identify your ideal customers more easily. The more you involve yourself in the process, the more you learn, and, obviously, the better and more proficient you will become at devising and assembling successful campaigns.

Don't be discouraged if a promotion you spent a lot of time on falls flat. In all reality, prepare yourself for it. Chances are it will happen at some point and you will have to deal with defeat. More likely than not, deflating occurrences happen as you are learning how to market and launch promotions, which makes the defeat seem larger than it really is.

Here is where your budget comes in and plays a key role in your game plan.

By not paying out too much money, actually any at all, you create a bumper of sorts, cushioning the loss and easing your burden. Yes, you spent a lot of time on the promotion, and yes, your time is money.

But also flip the coin and realize what you have learned.

Chances are, you have a pretty good idea of what not to do. Ask yourself the questions we discussed and see if there is room for changing up a couple of key components. Maybe email isn't all you hoped it would be, or maybe people aren't coming to your website as much as you thought they were.

Is there a small change you can make without having to plan an entire campaign?

Of course there is.

Often, we are lured into thinking a particular marketing path will be exactly the route to take. When reality hits, usually in the form of the sound of crickets, we'd be smart to take a step back and see if we were swayed by fancy sparkles and twirling lights.

There are many programs available promising 'do all promotions' and 'sell numbers' that would make Warren Buffet buy in. Facts are facts, and no matter the promise or the pitch, these 'do all' promises are like dust in the wind.

See if you can come up with one really good idea to pull more viewers to your website.

By writing a blog about your ideal customers' biggest pains and emotional struggles, this will attract their attention so you can give them the information they need.

Start a newsletter, just a one-page email, and discuss a recent experience you had that you think will be interesting (or entertaining!) to your industry. Maybe you'd feel better about sending it to one or two of your colleagues to see if it is as industry specific as you want it to be. Afterward, email it to everyone you know. Even if they aren't truckers, they may enjoy hearing about an adventure you had, or they may even share a laugh with you.

Strike up conversations at truck stops and regular places you frequent. See if anyone else has a story or maybe would like to contribute to your website. Make sure all information goes through you first; don't ever let anyone post directly on your site, even when responding with a comment or post.

There are 'bot sites' and destructive hackers who can cause all kinds of havoc, and securing your website is just one more thing you won't have to worry about. If you choose a responsible web host, they will have options for you to choose from, which will give you control over who has access and who doesn't.

With that said, let's review a few things you have learned reading this book:

- You have written a Mission Statement and Business Plan, along with an Executive Summary and Financial Estimates, which will not only be a welcome tool for accounting, but will be needed if you are looking for additional funding or partnerships.

- You have legally established your company and understand the necessity of properly setting boundaries between your personal assets and business liabilities to protect, not only property and assets, but also loved ones and family.

- You know and understand the business side of having a trucking business and are equipped with successful and proven strategy methods to make your company thrive.

- You know how to determine who your best customers are, how to find out where they congregate, and how to attract and retain their trust and business.

- You understand the reasons for evaluating a marketing plan and the benefits which can be found by actually doing so.

- You have either mastered or will master software apps which will make your business run smooth and soundly, even when you aren't there to monitor it.

- Most importantly, you understand the weight of having a satisfied customer, how their satisfaction can be turned into advertising for you, and how you both will benefit from engaging in a trusting and supportive relationship.

A final note on our current conditions and how this may affect our industry in the future.

None of us knows quite how long the COVID-19 pandemic effects might last or how far-reaching into the future they may go. Our industry has seen exponential growth, and, currently, many companies are setting up shop without having a clear grasp on what running a trucking company demands or what is required for it to be successful.

But one thing is clear.

You will be ahead of the crowd by using the methods stated in this book.

The pandemic crisis will be around for quite some time, either directly or indirectly with fallout and lasting circumstances. The businesses who survive and make money during this unpredictable time will be the businesses who can adapt, invent, show dependability, and create new avenues in which to run their companies and provide service to their customers. In other words, change won't keep you from working.

With the tools you have from this book, you also have the power to invent your future and create a sustainable lifestyle by comparing, analyzing, creating, testing, readjusting, and creating again. There is no perfect solution for everything. Within our communities, whether they reach across town or across the continent, we know this: by connecting on a common and engaging level, we go beyond just providing a service. We build relationships to stand the test of time which can weather any storm.

We are proud to be a part of the trucking and CDL operator's community.

And we hope you are too!

Thank you for being part of this foundational and vital industry. It started over a hundred years ago, and the industry promises to be around for at least a hundred years more. We don't know what innovations and technology will affect our industry, but as long as there's a need for long-haulers and drivers, there will be long-haulers here to do the job.

If you feel this book lived up to its promise and delivered more than you hoped for, we'd appreciate a favorable review. By sharing your positive reviews, this important information will rank higher in the lists, increase readership of like-minded drivers, and create a better informed industry and lifestyle for us all.

Thank you!

Special Bonus Offer: Free Gift for You! :)

Thank you! Here's a Free Gift! For You :)

As a special thanks from me to you, you'll receive:

- ❏ 3 Powerful Elements of Productivity in your Business
- ❏ 5 Simple Strategies to Mastering Productivity in your Business
- ❏ The Highest Quality of Productivity Charts
- ❏ Valuable Resources that you Must Know and much more!

To receive your Free copy of the CDL Business Productivity GAME PLAN, you can go to my website at:
cdlforlife.com/cdl-business-resources

SCAN ME
(For your Free Business Game Plan)

SCAN ME
(If you want my Books for Free)

Also If you would like to get my books for Free and before anyone else, go to my website at:
cdlforlife.com/cdl-business-resources

ADDITIONAL INFORMATION, HELPFUL INDUSTRY LINKS, SUGGESTED READING

Forums, Directories, and Online Communities

Class A Drivers - live forum

Expeditersonline

Team Run Smart - Freightliner

Truckers Report

Trucking Truth

Marketing Tools and Templates

12 Free Marketing Budget Templates

Software Designed Especially for Truckers

Publication Sources for Periodicals and Magazines

WebWire Publications

Samples of Good Trucking Business and Marketing Plans

B Plans

Profitable Venture - Sample Trucking Company Marketing Plan

**Support, Advice, and Information Articles
for CDL Business Operators**

ATBS

Commercial Capital LLC USA and Canada

Trade Shows, Conferences, and Social Events - *event information may be out of date due to the coronavirus (COVID-19). Confirm details with event organizers*

Drivewyze Trucking Events, Trade Shows, and Conferences

Triumph Business Capital Events List

Apps to Help You Do Your Job *Better & Effectively* **with Ease**

The following apps are available in Google Play Store and Apply Store, unless otherwise stated.

This app gives you the ability to log in your pre-trip, post trip, and driving hours:

Samsara Driver

This app enables you to track your fleet of vehicles your drivers are using:

Samsara Administrator - Fleet

The following two apps are for pre-trip and post-trip inspections to help drivers of small businesses and start-ups save costs and time:

DVIR 2.0 Pre-Trip Inspection

Keep Truckin' Driver - ELD

(The following are ratings and opinions by Smart Trucking - Great Apps for Truckers and More[1], Smart Trucking, who also conducted the testing.)

Whether you are on the road or in the office, we all can use an extra hand now and then.

Well, these aren't extra hands, but they certainly can make your life a bit easier, by either giving you more time, supporting your business, or entertaining you along the way.

All these apps have been tested, both on Android and iPhone devices. Not all of these apps are specifically for drivers, but if they aren't, rest assured, after our test we thought they would be of great benefit. Ratings are on a 5-star system, and none of these listed are below a 4-star rating. They all can be found on both the Apple Store and the Google Play Store.

If you find one or several to not be of your liking, please consider, we've done our best to give you some great stuff. If it (they) aren't great or the app isn't available, please delete, but don't hold us accountable. These apps are updated and change often - what was good today may not be worth 2¢ tomorrow!

BEST ALL IN ONE TRUCKER APP
TRUCKER PATH

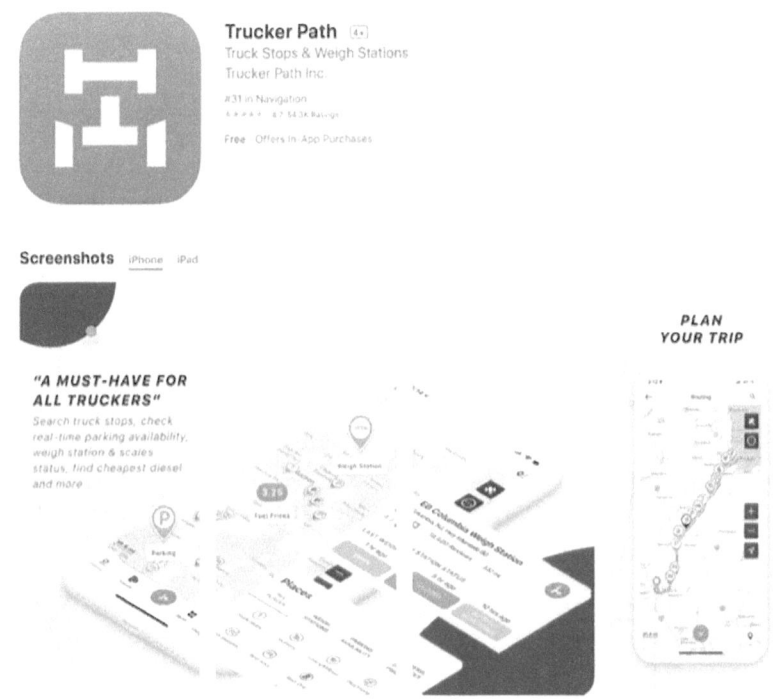

- Lists more than 7000 truck stops in the USA and Canada

- Updates on parking availability

- Truck drivers' forum

- Information on weigh station and scales

- Trip planner option

- Plenty of job listings

- Find fuel stops with truck clearance

- Saves your navigation history

- Helps to find your next truck

- Advanced address search

Trucker Plus has a user-friendly interface and it gives you all the relevant information you would expect.

The Trucker Path comes with a unique mapping system you can use to avoid low bridges and find the nearest fuel stops with truck clearance.

It shows the nearest parking locations including, Walmarts, where you can often park overnight.

You can use the app to compare fuel prices and record hours of service.

You can check on weigh stations and scales.

What makes Trucker Path different from most trucking apps is its huge community; it has more than 800,000 active users in North America. You can chat with other drivers on the truck forum, apply for truck driving jobs, and even search for trucks for sale.

NOTE: The navigation on Trucker Path is not as advanced, compared to specialized GPS units. It can plan routes and find good gas prices, but precise navigation details are not the best-selling points. Stay with the premium GPS units. It also needs internet connections to navigate.

BEST TRUCKER FUEL APP
GAS BUDDY

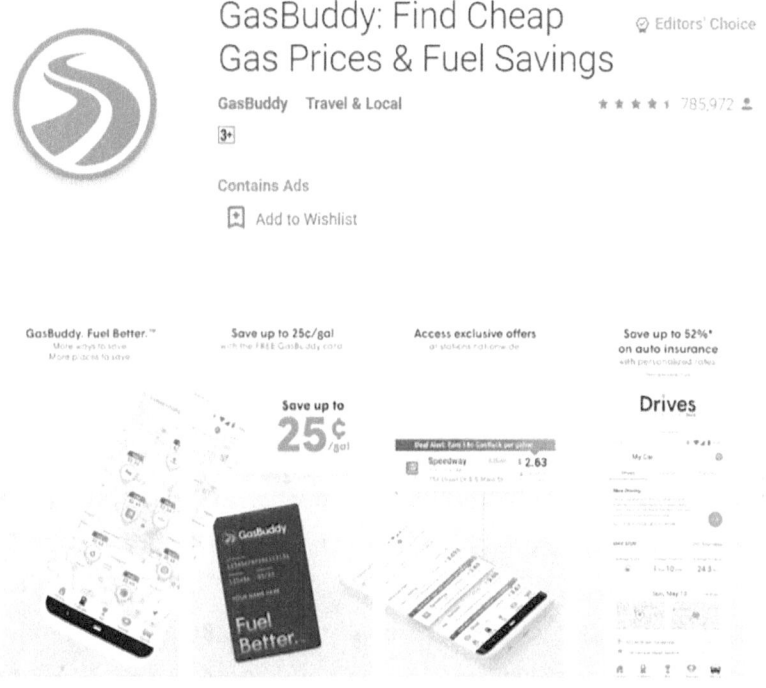

- Includes more than 150,000 gas stations in North America

- Helps to find the cheapest fuel price

- Offers fuel rewards

- Access gas station and store review

- It tells you when you're wasting fuel

- Information on fuel stops with shower and food

Gas Buddy is a free app available on both Android and iPhone.

With a database listing of more than 150,000 fuel stations across North America, finding the cheapest fuel prices is easy.

This app notifies you when the price of diesel is about to increase, so you can fill up your tank before it happens.

It can also monitor your driving habits and inform you when you're wasting gas and money.

Since GasBuddy has thousands of users, you can find reviews for fuel stations and convenience stores along your route.

You may be rewarded with free gas coupons if you pay for items at Walmart, Amazon, Home Depot, or other major retailers using the GasBuddy app or card.

Although Gas Buddy is technically a fuel-saving app, it can inform you where to find fuel stops with food and showers.

BEST SATELLITE AND STREET VIEWS APP
GOOGLE MAPS

Maps - Navigate & Explore

Google LLC   Travel & Local

3+

Contains Ads

Add to Wishlist

⊘ Editors' Choice

★ ★ ★ ★ ⅰ   11,682,364 ▲

Install

- Panorama street view

- Satellite view to check parking spots

- Real-time traffic updates

- Updates on businesses that are open and closed

- Discover restaurants, fuel stations, and rest areas

- Saves your search history

- Voice assistance feature (important for truck drivers)

Google Maps is not really an exclusive trucker app, but the satellite and street view feature can be amazingly helpful.

The satellite view allows you to see a property from an overhead position, giving you a heads up on any obstructions, so you will know which driveway to follow, and where to find the dock.

You can switch to street-view easily, to get a 360-degree angle view of different locations on the map, just as you would see it if you're driving on the road in your truck.

Google Maps makes it possible for you to see exactly how a location looks before you arrive at the destination, eliminating any surprises.

You can receive real-time traffic updates and discover points of interest.

In case you're wondering, you can activate voice assistance to give you directions while your eyes are focused on the road (where they belong!) This app doesn't prioritize truck routes.

BEST PRECLEARANCE APP
DRIVEWYZE

Drivewyze PreClear Trucker App

Drivewyze Inc.   Maps & Navigation

★ ★ ★ ★ 1,369

3+

Add to Wishlist

Drivewyze offers more bypasses in mor

Drivewyze provides bypasses in 47 states and provinces

- Helps you to bypass weigh stations

- Approved by over 40 states in the USA

- 30-day free trial

- Receive alerts when you're close to an inspection site or a weigh station

- User-friendly interface How much time do you waste on an inspection site or a weigh station?

On average, 30 minutes to an hour can be wasted on a single weigh station.

The Drivewyze app allows you to legally bypass weigh stations. The company behind it has a preclearance network of at least 700 sites across 44 states and provinces of the United States, and Canada.

If you're using a transponder bypass system, you can integrate it with the app and you will receive alerts at least 2 miles away from inspection sites and weigh stations that have a green-light both your transponder service and Drivewyze.

The app runs in the background and it doesn't require constant interaction, so you can concentrate on driving.

Not all inspection sites and weigh stations are connected to its network, though you will still receive an alert whenever you're near an inspection site or weigh station.

Drivewyze monthly subscription fee is $17.99 but you can get a free trial for the first 30 days. Certainly worth a try to see if it makes your life easier as a truck driver.

PREPASS MOTION

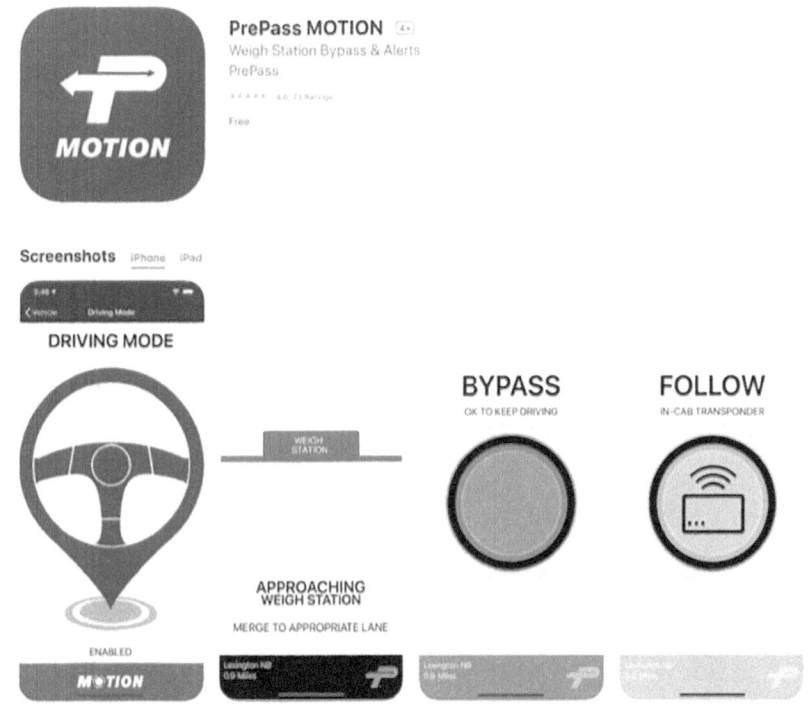

- Pre-clearance for weigh stations

- Helps to save fuel and money

- The app can be paired with a transponder

- Wide network coverage

- Fast customer care

The PrePass Motion is an alternative to Drivewyze, and can be used for pre-clearance purposes.

According to PrePass Motion, the app integrates with the in-cab transponder and Advance Vehicle Identification (AVI) reader, so you can continue driving on the main road without stopping at a weigh scale (this is an untested feature).

If you come across a weigh station without transponder readers, the app uses motion mobile sensors to receive and send the signals.

PrePass MOTION pre-clearance network is available in 42 states across the USA, including Alaska.

Additionally, in California, you can bypass 37 weigh stations and inspection sites using the app.

Users enjoy a toll payment service in most states.

Like Drivewyze, you won't get a pass in all weigh stations nationwide.

It doesn't cover Canada, if you cross the border.

It's free service up to some point, but if you want to enjoy certain privileges, you have to pay the subscription fees.

BEST MOBILE SCANNING APP
TRANSFLO MOBILE

TRANSFLO Mobile+
Pegasus TransTech

Free

- You can chat with dispatch

- Accept or decline loads

- Find trailer location

- Tells you weather conditions

- Updates the fuel stops and rest areas along your route

- Mobile scanning option

- It alerts when you approach a weigh station

- Supports hours of service

- Notifies you of payments made

Transflo Mobile is one of the best mobile scanning apps in the trucking industry; although technically, it does more than just scan, send, and receive documents.

You can chat back and forth with your carrier, dispatcher, or broker on the app.

You have an option to reject or accept loads. Once you arrive at your destination, you can confirm pick up delivery via the app.

Fleet managers who have installed T-Series ELD devices on trucks and trailers can use the app to track their location on the map.

Moreover, the app can track when the truck is moving so it can automatically record the hours of service, though to do that, it still needs to be integrated with the T-Series ELD devices.

As soon as you finish a job, collect the needed signatures, take a picture of the documents, and submit it for billing, all through the app. Since you're sending the paperwork on your smartphone, you will be paid faster.

After the payment comes through, the Transflo Mobile app will notify you. Beyond that, you can send photos when reporting an accident or OS&D submission to carriers.

The app can also alert you when approaching a weigh station and show you the fuel stops and rest areas along your route.

Once again, it doesn't navigate better than a dedicated truck GPS. But if you want to scan documents, it will do the job just fine.

BEST TRIP PLANNING APP
PILOT FLYING J

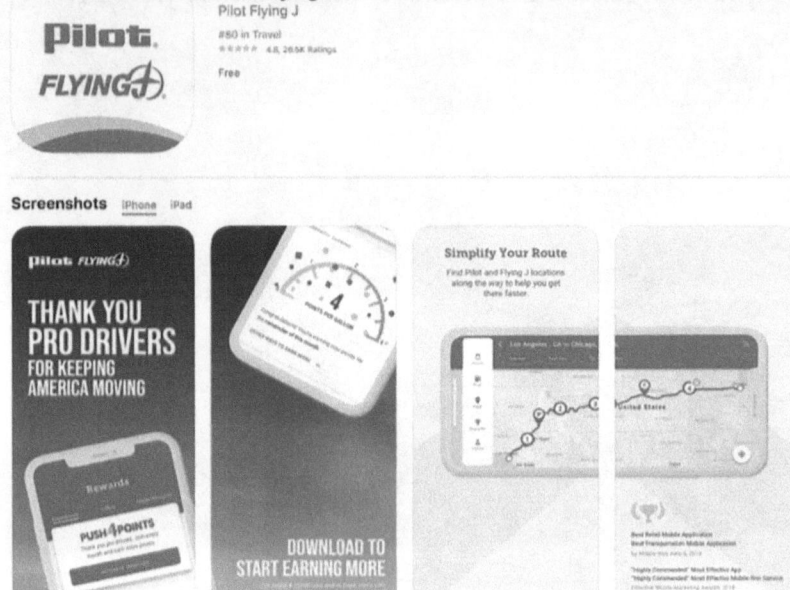

- Free shower rewards

- Access to parking spaces

- Reserve your shower spot at a location

- Free meal on your birthday

- Redeem your points for discounts

- Free drink after signing up

- Reserve a parking spot

- Saves digital receipts

- Mobile fueling option

- Information on available amenities

Before the Pilot Flying J app was launched, the team behind it did a survey and asked many professional truckers what they would like in an app to help their road planning become easier.

Interestingly, most truckers said they would enjoy a free shower; and even if their shower credit expires, they shouldn't worry about it too much.

The outcome was a trip planning app that offers members free daily shower rewards after redeeming re-fueling points.

Otherwise, you can reserve your shower and parking spot using the app, so you avoid wasting time if you're in a hurry (which is more likely than not the case for a truck driver)!

For what it's worth, most Pilot and Flying J locations have reasonably clean showers.

You will get offers and discounts every time you pass through their truck stops. Buy one, get one free, or maybe free coffee. Did I mention, you get a free meal on your birthday?

You can use the mobile fueling option to fill out the fuel pump prompts in advance. In addition, the app shares information about the amenities available at nearby locations. It can tell you what type of food is available, the number of parking spots open, number of showers, and truck assistance services in specified locations.

You can, however, only access those free showers, parking spots, and special discounts at Pilot and Flying J locations. With 750 Pilot Flying J locations across North America, though, it isn't too hard to find one enroute.

LOVE'S CONNECT

Love's Connect

Love's Travel Stops and Country Stores, Inc.   Shopping ★ ★ ★ ★ · 24,203 ▲
3+

🔖 Add to Wishlist

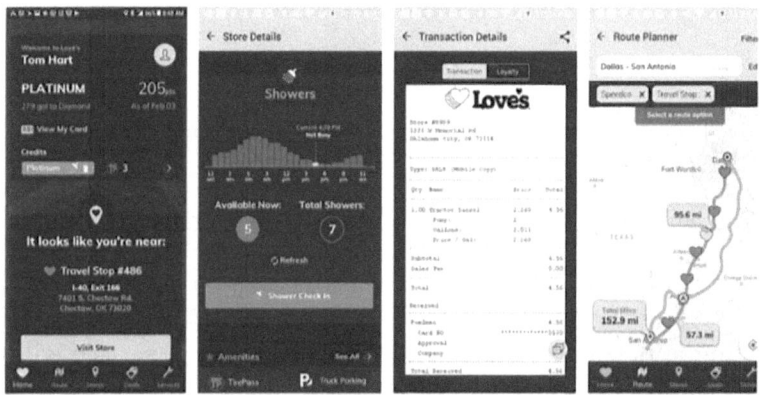

- Helps locate the nearest LOVE'S truck stop

- You can redeem points for rewards

- It saves digital receipts

- Check fuel prices along your route

- Activate the pump from your phone

- Shower check-in feature

If you prefer a different trip planning app than Pilot Flying J, Love's Connect is a good alternative; maybe you can use both.

You can use the app to get location pins on the nearest Love's truck stops.

Once you arrive at any Love's travel stop, you can book a shower slot using your smartphone.

You will receive points after every refuel at Love's truck stops.

You can redeem the points to shop for items or free showers. Keep in mind, when you reach Platinum status, *your points will triple.*

You can check for competitive fuel prices along your route.

Though Love's Connect ticks almost all the boxes for the best trip planning app, parking spaces fill up fast. Customer service will make you a priority, though, if you use the app.

BEST AUDIOBOOK APP
AUDIBLE

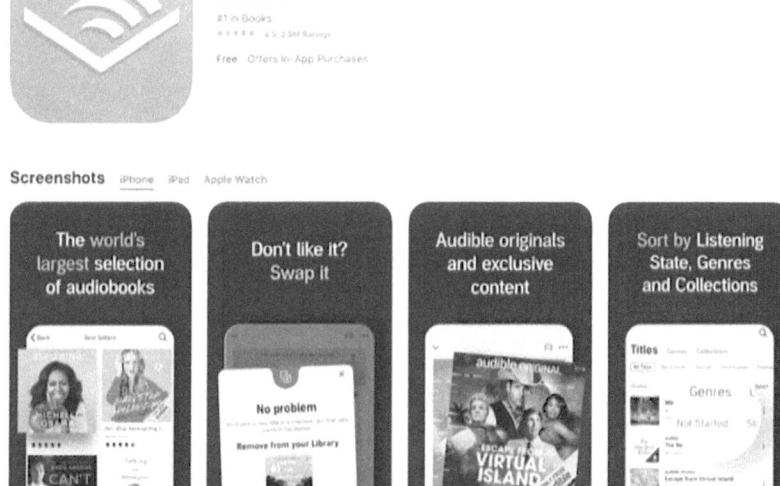

- Wide collection of audiobooks

- Customize your library

- Listen to audiobooks offline

- Sign in with Amazon account

- User-friendly interface

- Free first-month trial

If you want to listen to audiobooks in your truck, Audible gives you access to thousands of titles.

Users sign in with their Amazon account. If you're a new member, you receive a 30-day free trial.

After the free trial expires, your account will be billed $14.95 per month. However, if you're an Amazon Prime member, you will receive discounts and free Audible content.

For easy navigation, the content is categorized into different genres and collections. You also have access to the 'bestseller' lists for the New York Times, Amazon, etc.

You can personalize your library and download the audiobooks to listen offline.

You won't receive many free goodies after the first month, but considering Audible has the world's largest catalog of audiobooks, the subscription fees seem reasonable.

BEST MUSIC STREAMING APP
SPOTIFY

Spotify: Music and Podcasts [12+]
Discover the latest songs
Spotify Ltd.

#1 in Music
★★★★★ 4.8 12.3M Ratings

Free Offers In-App Purchases

- Good audio quality

- Create your playlist

- Easy to search interface

- Integrate with other devices

- Free version available

Spotify is the biggest music streaming service at the moment with a catalog of more than 50 million songs and 700,000 podcasts. Its huge library makes it perfect to listen to music on the road without getting bored.

Users can choose the free version available with adverts or the premium version with no ads.

As might be expected, there is a 1-month free trial if you have never paid for premium.

You can access Spotify on any device with Windows, Android, macOS, and iOS. You can also create playlists. If you choose to discontinue your premium membership, you will lose access to your playlists and any content you may have downloaded.

BEST APP FOR RELAXATION
CALM RADIO

Calm Radio - Music to Relax
500 Channels for Relaxation
Calm Radio

★ ★ ★ ★ ★ 4.5, 16K Ratings

Free · Offers In-App Purchases

Screenshots iPhone iPad Apple TV

- Lots of music channels

- Meditation music

- Sleep timer

- Equalizer tone controls

- Nature sounds in the background

- Unlimited listening

- Free membership with ads

This app is convenient when you're on a break and you probably want to sleep or meditate. You know, recharge your batteries before the next trip?

The app comes with more than 500 HD audio channels to stream relaxation music. If you want a free membership, the channels will have ads, a bit disturbing if you are in the middle of a meditation. Otherwise, you'll need to pay a slight membership fee, which is very worth it.

Besides listening to all types of relaxing genres like Jazz, classical music, country music, pop-rock, and adult contemporary, you can choose to play nature sounds in the background, which are very true to life. You feel like you are at the beach or in the forest. Better yet, you can listen to binaural beat therapy and set up a sleep timer.

This is one of my favorite apps and is quite reasonably priced for the premium version if you watch for their occasional deals (I paid $70 CDN for an entire year). Excellent value.

BEST FITNESS APP FOR TRUCKERS
ROLLING STRONG

Rolling Strong [17+]
Driving Good Health
Stephen Kane
★★★★★ 4.7 • 15 Ratings
Free · Offers In-App Purchases

Screenshots   iPhone   iPad

  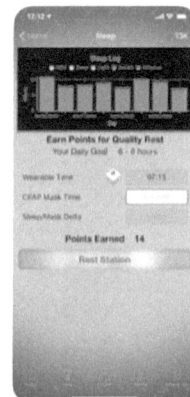 

- It tells you nearest fitness spots

- Monitors your sleeping pattern

- Helps track your calories

- Redeem points for rewards

- Online coaching to get fit

- Reminds you to hydrate

Once you sign up to the app, its AI will guide you to create a diet and a workout plan to fit your goals.

Beyond that, the app will monitor your sleeping pattern and remind you when it's time to hydrate.

Since you will be on the road frequently, the app will show you the nearest fitness spots with truck parking spaces available based on your locations. Alternatively, you can watch exercise training videos and consult with fitness coaches through the app to help you work out if you can't find a gym.

To enjoy the full perks of the Rolling Strong app, you need to pay a monthly membership fee of $4.99. That's cheap for a fitness app with an assistant coach.

In a nutshell, all the apps on this list are ideal for truck drivers and compatible with Android and iPhones. Of course, you don't need to clutter your smartphone with too many apps, just use the ones you think you will benefit from.

Above everything else, keep your hands away from the phone when you're driving. If you must engage an app when you're at the wheel, make sure your smartphone is mounted on the dashboard and you can activate voice assistance.

SUGGESTED READING

Progressive Business Plan for an Independent Trucking Company: A Detailed Template System with Innovative Growth Strategies

Setting up an independent trucking company is heavily dependent on having the right plan and a strategic vision. These are the aspects of a business setup that the book will address.

Online Advertising Made Simple - Trucking

The focus here is specifically on digital marketing and how it could be beneficial for a trucking or CDL company.

CDL Minded Entrepreneur: 3-Step System to Leverage Time, Have Unlimited Freedom and Maximize Security in the CDL Industry

This book provides excellent guidance and the overall CDL mindset on starting and building a successful business.

REFERENCES

[1] MacMillan, C. *The best trucker apps 2020 – for on + off the road.* Smart Trucking. https://www.smart-trucking.com/trucker-apps/

[2] Truckernews.com. Truckers favor Facebook which turns 15 today. https://www.truckersnews.com/survey-truckers-favor-facebook-which-turns-15-today/

[3] Bureau of Labor Statistics.News release.National census of fatal occupational injuries in 2018. 12/17/2019. https://www.bls.gov/news.release/pdf/cfoi.pdf

[10] Best Web Hosting Services. (2020). https://hostingfacts.com/

[11] Best Free Website Builders. (2020). https://www.websitebuild erexpert.com/website-builders/best/free/

Thank you for your Honest Experience :)

Thank you! I hope this brings you great value as it did for me sharing my story with you.

My purpose and mission is to guide and encourage you to become the best version of yourself in your life by providing everything you need to achieve your dreams for yourself, your family and your business.

However, in order to do that, sharing your honest review on **amazon** (or Audible) helps spread the word to other CDL Minded friends (like yourself) and will help many readers who are struggling to make their dreams become a reality.

If you do have 30 secs to leave a **1-Click honest review,** I greatly appreciate it because it shows that you're not like most people.

It means that you truly value yourself in what you do. It also means that you're CDL Minded in yourself, your family and in your business.

I truly appreciate all your love and support and I'm thankful and grateful for your life and I greatly value your honest opinion and thoughts. :)

If you need anything, feel free to reach out at my website and to receive your Free Gift if you haven't received it yet.

You can also share your experience by taking a photo of this book and attach it to the review so other CDL Minded friends can be inspired and encouraged from your honest experience.
SCAN ME!

Just One Click (once you click on this review page or scan QR Code):

When you finish, just Click Submit at the bottom of the page and that's it. Please click on this link or scan the QR code to **Review Book on Amazon!**

Overall rating
☆ ☆ ☆ ☆ ☆

Add a headline
What's most important to know?

Add a photo or video
Shoppers find images and videos more helpful than text alone.
+

Add a written review
What did you like or dislike? What did you use this product for?

Submit

Looking forward to working together and helping you achieve your goals. Take care and talk to you soon! :)

www.ingramcontent.com/pod-product-compliance
Lightning Source LLC
Chambersburg PA
CBHW021709120626
46545CB00004B/1481